# YOU CAN TEACH YOURSELF®

# HAMMERED DULCIMER

## by Madeline MacNeil

## PHOTO CREDITS

Page 3:   Photo by Laurie Bridgeforth.
Page 5:   Photos courtesy Dusty Strings Dulcimer Company.
Page 6:   Top photos by Bonnie Jacobs.
          Bottom photo courtesy Dusty Strings Dulcimer Company.
Page 7:   Photos by Bonnie Jacobs.
Page 8:   Photos by Bonnie Jacobs.
Page 21:  Photo by Bonnie Jacobs.

## Audio Contents

| | | |
|---|---|---|
| 1  Introduction [:45] | 12  Harvest Home [1:56] | 23  Soldier's Joy [1:37] |
| 2  Counting Off [:25] | 13  Annie Laurie [1:46] | 24  The Parting Glass [1:24] |
| 3  Key of G [3:19] | 14  No Place Like Home [1:45] | 25  Star of the Country Down [1:18] |
| 4  Are You Sleeping? [:57] | 15  Interval Exercise, Key of G [1:02] | 26  Simple Gifts [1:27] |
| 5  O Susanna [1:41] | 16  Deck the Halls [1:18] | 27  Flop-Eared Mule [1:53] |
| 6  Go Tell Aunt Rhody [:42] | 17  Back-Up Chords [2:31] | 28  Over the Waterfall [1:28] |
| 7  Hammering Exercises in the Key of G [2:09] | 18  Auld Lang Syne [1:49] | 29  The Ash Grove [1:28] |
| 8  Golden Slippers [1:33] | 19  My Own House [2:23] | 30  Planxty Fanny Po'er [2:12] |
| 9  Home On The Range [1:34] | 20  The Lark in the Clear Air [1:26] | 31  The Hundred Pipers [1:16] |
| 10  Arkansas Traveler [1:17] | 21  Amazing Grace [1:15] | 32  Santa Lucia [1:36] |
| 11  Liberty [2:21] | 22  Off to California [1:42] | 33  Jesu, Joy of Man's Desiring [3:39] |

**Online Audio & Video**

**Audio**
www.melbay.com/95440EB

**Video**
dv.melbay.com/95440

**YouTube**
www.melbay.com/95440V

*WWW.MELBAY.COM*

# Contents

# Dedication

In no way was this book an individual effort! My grateful thanks go to Tabby Finch, Pat McKelvy, Marilyn Lister, Mary Lautzenheimer and Seth Austen for their technical help; to Clare Ellis for managing my work so I had time to write; to my friends Sam and Carrie Rizzetta, Stephanie Cochran, Connie Evans, Brad Stoller, Janita Baker, Sue Mohrs, René Poirier, and Rick Thum; to Bonnie Jacobs and Dusty Strings Instruments for the photographs; to Robert Barnes for always being there; and to my beloved dulcimer students who teach me so much.

# About the Author

Madeline MacNeil is well known for her talents as a gifted singer and performer on the hammered and mountain dulcimers. She is probably equally well known for the warmth and generosity with which she shares her music and encourages others to play and sing. Maddie's teaching has taken her to the Augusta Heritage Arts Workshops at Davis and Elkins College in Elkins, West Virginia; to the Dulcimer Playing Workshop at Appalachian State University in Boone, North Carolina; and to festivals throughout the country. The silver-haired woman with the golden voice has won the admiration of countless fans across the country.

*Madeline MacNeil.*

# Introduction

Congratulations on your decision to make a hammered dulcimer part of your musical life! You'll find good music, good people and good festivals for encouragement along the way. I began playing the hammered dulcimer in 1979, having discovered it a few years before. It is a delight to play, and an instrument I enjoy sharing with others. For many years I've taught dulcimer in workshops and at festivals. This book is a result of my teaching and learning from other players and students whose enthusiasm match my own. It is a privilege to work with you.

This book begins with tuning tips and scales, then continues with arrangements to help you with skill building. Some of the tunes are standards at old-time music jams while others are favorites of players of all kinds of instruments. Guitar chords accompany all of the arrangements except one, and I hope you'll find someone to join in the music.

# If You Read Music

Some sections of the book are designed for those who read music slowly — or hardly at all. You, as a music reader, will have no problem knowing G is G. However, the hammered dulcimer has its own playing style, and this may slow your learning, especially if you play keyboards. Quite simply, instead of notes (low to high) progressing left to right horizontally — as they do on a keyboard — they go right to left horizontally, vertically and diagonally! Also, there are duplicated notes; D above middle C is found on the right side of the treble bridge and also on the bass bridge, for example.

Confusion will disappear eventually. I remember, early on, trying to play a simple classical tune on the dulcimer from a piano book. At one point, I held the hammers over the instrument thinking, "Let's see. The bass is on the right..." Today I switch easily from keyboard to dulcimer, as do other players.

Your biggest hurdle might involve learning to play by ear and creating your own arrangements. I suggest you put written music aside as soon as possible (sooner than you think it is possible). Learn four measures of a tune, then play without looking at the music. It is easier to keep an eye on the dulcimer when there's no sheet music to distract you. Trust any instincts to modify the written music. Music is alive and you are part of the process.

# If You Read Music S-L-O-W-L-Y Or Not At All

Music reading is a nice skill to have. If you feel strongly that some of the best players of traditional music can't read a note, you're right. However, I've heard some of them explain a chord or melodic line in a language all their own. They know what they're doing! Written music is simply a means of communication, a way to express musical ideas, a second language. It is a logical, mathematical language. *You* provide the creative expression.

Every tune in this book has the name of the notes under the music. If you see D, and your dulcimer has low D's, mid-range D's and high D's, which D is it? The position of the note on the staff (the five lines and four spaces) will help you. Does the *physical* position of the note lie high, low or in the middle? Simply, notes high or low on the staff (or on extending ledger lines) are high and low on the dulcimer. Notes on the middle of the staff are mid-range notes.

I encourage music readers in the section above to memorize small portions of a tune as they learn it. I encourage you to do the same thing — for different reasons. Measure after measure of musical notation can be intimidating. If you get the "sense" of two or three or four measures, playing them by ear and memory, the rest of the tune will fall into place more easily.

The available video will reinforce the musical arrangements for you. Ultimately, those of us who play by ear find a good home in folk music. Music reading and playing by ear, in combination, open up a vast world of good music.

# Dulcimer Layout
# or: Where The Notes Are

Sets of strings tuned to the same pitch and running parallel so they are struck simultaneously are called courses. Most modern dulcimers use two- and three-string courses, although four-string courses were common on older instruments.

You'll hear dulcimers described as "12/11" or "15/14." That means 12 courses on the treble bridge and 11 courses on the bass bridge, or 15 courses on the treble bridge and 14 courses on the bass bridge. You'll also

hear about chromatic dulcimers, three-octave for example. This means all of the notes between D below middle C, usually, and D two octaves above middle C are available somewhere on the instrument. I play an extended range dulcimer with a range of four octaves, most of them chromatic.

Because dulcimers are hand-crafted, leaning to the whims and creativity of the builders, anything is possible. Most typical are the 12/11 and 15/14 dulcimers, and this book will address those instruments. In all probability, however, the book is adaptable to your instrument, should it not be a 12/11 or 15/14.

*12/11 hammered dulcimer.*

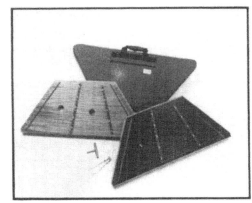

*15/14 hammered dulcimer.*

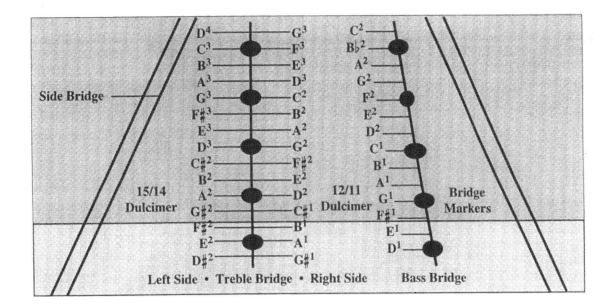

*This 12/11 dulcimer is on a stand where the player stands. Notice how the instrument is tilted just a little at the bottom edge. This stand is not adjustable.*

*This chromatic, extended-range dulcimer is angled more for sitting. (For the photograph, the stand was raised a little.) Notice this is an adjustable stand.*

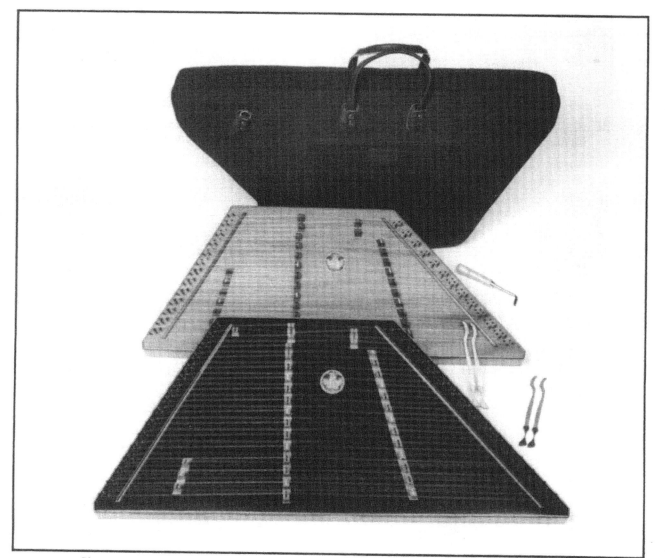

*Chromatic hammered dulcimers. Notice offset bridges and the third bridge on the far left.*

# Hammers

Wooden hammers are the connection between you and the strings. Some hammers are "spoon-shaped," others are double-sided; many variations on these shapes are available. Hammers with pads (leather, felt, etc.) and those with bare wood produce slightly different tone qualities.

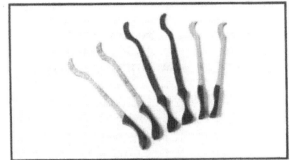

*Single-sided hammers. Notice the variations in the gripping-ends.*

*Double-sided hammers. Notice the different shapes*

Most hammers are rigid, but you'll find flexible ones which are especially suited for use on the cousins of the hammered dulcimer, such as the cymbalom, when tremolo (rapid vibrato) is desired.

At a festival or workshop, be curious about other hammers. Borrow a set to try on your dulcimer. Some people swear by a shorter shaft; others (like me) prefer longer ones. Some people like lighter hammers; others heavier ones. I find slightly heavier hammers easier to control. Balance is critical to your playing. Is the hammer heavier on the head-end? Gripping-end? I prefer ones that almost work like a see-saw in my hand.

And finally, the gripping-end should be comfortable. If your hammers slip in your hands or generally feel uncomfortable, look for another pair. Chefs have *their* knives; painters have *their* brushes; gardeners have *their* rakes and hoes; you have *your* hammers. The hammers are your tools for playing the instrument, and they must be right for you.

# Bridges

The word "bridge" covers two parts of the dulcimer: A treble bridge and a bass bridge. The treble bridge contains the mid- and high-range notes; the bass bridge contains the low-range notes. (Your instrument may have another short bridge on the far left.) The courses of strings cross over the bridges.

# Marked Bridges

Without markings (a different color) on some bridges, the dulcimer is a sea of strings. These days most dulcimers have black or white bridges strategically placed to guide you. The marks indicate where major (Do-Re-Mi) scales begin, and they also help you find your way quickly. If your dulcimer has no markings, I implore you to change that. Some Peel n' Stick dots of various colors (found at a stationery store) will do. For where to place them, refer to your instrument's tuning chart or to the diagrams of dulcimers throughout the book.

*On this dulcimer the marked bridges are white. This is a chromatic dulcimer. Notice the offset bridges at the top. For some needed notes on a chromatic dulcimer, bridges are moved to shorten or lengthen the string.*

# Tuning your dulcimer

## Helpful Devices

Although dulcimer players have tuned for centuries using just their ears, two tools are now available that simplify the task considerably: an electronic tuner and a device to isolate the sound of your strings.

**The Electronic Tuner:** Some have lights, some have dials, some have both. No matter what they have, they indicate how close you are to a desired pitch. Example — using a dial when tuning a string to D: You pluck the string (using your fingernail or a guitar pick), and the dial indicates your pitch is lower than D. You turn the tuning wrench on the pin of that string, slowly and carefully, generally clockwise, until the dial indicates the D-pitch is right-on. If you overshoot D, a slight turn (probably counter-clockwise) will bring it back. An electronic tuner is infinitely better than using a piano or your ear for help in tuning the dulcimer.

Electronic tuners can be found in music stores and through folk music catalogs. There are a variety of styles — some with bells and whistles — and prices. Shop around; ask for demonstrations when possible. One cautionary note: you *must* have a chromatic tuner. A guitar tuner (with only six notes) is *not* for you.

**The Tuner-Helper:** Suppose you are tuning in a room where several other players are tuning up. Suppose your kids are talking, laughing, and playing the stereo — four rooms away! The tuner is unable to isolate the sound of your string, so the dial is jumping and lights are flashing. A wire (I call it a Tuner-Helper) plugs into the tuner and clamps onto a tuning pin on the dulcimer. The tuner then hears only you. *You do not have to move the clamp every time you tune a new note.* I highly recommend you get one after you've gotten a tuner. One can be built from components found at Radio Shack. I bought one from Ed Hale (700 West "D" Street, N. Little Rock, AR 72116).

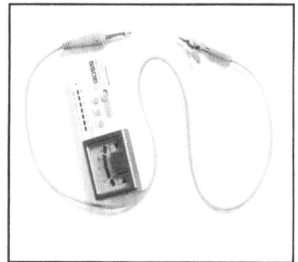
*A typical electronic tuner and a tuner-helper.*

**The Tuning Wrench:** After your large investment in purchasing a dulcimer, here I'm telling you to spend more money. However, I mention things that I feel are necessary for your learning comfort. Satin-lined dulcimer cases are up to you!

Feel a tuning pin on the dulcimer: It is square. Look at the tip of your tuning wrench. If it is square ■ please buy another wrench (not a large expense). Square wrenches don't fit snugly on the pins and, over time, can round the pins. You can't turn a round pin. You want a star-tipped wrench ✸. These grip the pins snugly.

There are goose-neck wrenches and T-handle wrenches. As long as they have star-tipped ends, both are fine. The goose-neck wrench, with its distance from the pin, has a better torque and makes tuning a little easier.

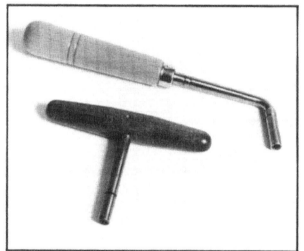
*Goose-neck and T-handle tuning wrenches.*

A quiet spot is preferable, of course. Until you learn all of the notes on the instrument, you need the tuning scheme given to you by the builder. You also need something to give you the necessary reference pitches: an electronic tuner (my preference, as you can guess), a piano, or a pitch pipe.

Begin at the lowest note on the right side of the treble bridge — probably a C# or G#. Work slowly with the tuning wrench, making sure the wrench is on the correct tuning pin! Determine which way tunes the note higher (generally clockwise), which way lower (generally counter-clockwise).

*Dulcimer tuning pins do not have to be moved much to raise or lower the pitch.* In fact, if you are turning the wrench and nothing is happening, stop! Make sure you're on the correct pin.

When the note on the right side of the treble bridge is tuned, tune the note opposite it on the left side. Usually only a little adjusting is necessary. If you're having trouble getting the two sides of the bridge to coordinate (the C# is fine, but the G# is off, for example), move the strings slightly on the bridge cap. This releases some tension on the strings, helping you tune each note. If you have consistent problems with the right and left sides of the bridge not coordinating, consult the builder or a piano technician for help.

Work your way up the treble bridge, then tune the notes on the bass bridge. When you finish, play some of the notes in different areas together (G's an octave apart, for example) and adjust when necessary. After you've gotten the knack of tuning, tuning all of the strings for the same note — all Cs on the instrument, then all C#s, then all Ds, etc.— may help you learn your dulcimer "keyboard" more quickly.

It may be tempting to tune only a few notes in the middle of the instrument or only ones you need to play a particular tune. Don't yield to temptation; there are many reasons to have the entire instrument in tune:

• Every time you strike a string, other strings in tune (or the harmonics of that string) vibrate, contributing to a lovely fullness.
• Strings kept in tune are easier to tune in the long run.
• Every time you tune, you are learning more about your instrument — sounds of the strings, the feel of the tuning wrench and the location of notes frequently and infrequently used.

I know it takes you a long time to tune at first, and I sympathize. My first attempts resembled the preparation and detail required for an appendectomy. Remember two things: Playing *for yourself* on a slightly out-of-tune dulcimer is no crime; but will be a lot less satisfying than playing one that's *in* tune.

## The Dulcimer Stand

You'll find stands for sitting, stands for standing, and stands adaptable for both sitting and standing. Your preference is your guide. My only comment is that you must be comfortable. Unfortunately, some of your first clues concerning poor dulcimer placement might be cricks in the neck and twinges in the back. Sitting or standing, adjust the tilt of the stand so you can reach higher notes comfortably. Preferences for the instrument stand are individualistic; what is comfortable for me might not be for you. Experiment.

Now comes the question: should one stand or sit to play the dulcimer? I'm going to throw that right back at you by saying, "You should either sit or stand while playing," although I know a couple of wonderful players who kneel by the instrument, which is on the floor. A person standing has more freedom to move around, an important factor in good playing. However, if you want to think ahead, an audience can better see what you're doing if you sit at the instrument. Again, comfort is a deciding factor. I do prefer that you sit or stand centered by the treble bridge (the long bridge to your left). This means you'll be a little left of center of the instrument, but centered on the treble bridge, where you do most of your playing.

## Playing In Comfort

You've heard of repetitive motion injuries, and you don't want them. Anything that adds tension to your playing is not good. Earlier we spoke of the position of the dulcimer on the stand. Also, be aware, periodically, of the hammers and how you're holding them. Do not *grip* them! Hold them loosely in your hands (at first they might feel as though they'll fall out). Do not play for extended periods of time without taking a break. Get up, walk around, stretch, wiggle your fingers, and think about something else for a bit.

# Playing in Rhythm
# Counting Off

Music readers will have no problem knowing quarter notes from eighth notes. But all of us can trip over complex rhythms—odd combinations of notes that have to felt to be understood.

A basic music book will give you details about rhythmic notation — what a time signature is, how many eighth notes it takes to equal a quarter note, and so forth. We will concentrate on bringing rhythmic notation to life.

For most of our musical lives, we've counted, "one–two–and–three–and–four" to denote a measure consisting of a quarter note, two eighth notes, two eighth notes and a quarter note. It works, but sometimes words can help also. How about "walk" for quarter notes; "run" and "running" for eighth notes; and "hold" for half, dotted half, and whole notes?

Getting a good rhythmic start when playing the dulcimer is very important. Each piece in the book will get you started by having you verbally count yourself in.

*Count Off: 1-2 Ready Play*

In this example, the music starts on the 1st beat of the measure.

---

*Count Off: 1 Ready Play*

In this example, the music starts on the 4th beat of the measure (what we also call an upbeat).

---

A metronome is a good tool to help you keep a tune rhythmical and to build speed. Also, electric keyboards found in many homes have interesting drum patterns at varying speeds and accents. You might find working with an electric keyboard more fun.

People who continually sing or play music alone are prone to uneven, sometimes sloppy, rhythm. Trust me; I'm a solo performer! A metronome is almost essential for us. A music store will have a variety of models and prices from which to choose.

There are metronome markings (♩=112, for example) at the beginning of each tune. These are generally speeds to which you aim when you can play through the tune.

# Playing Tunes

At first, getting through a few tunes is more important than playing with expressive beauty! Our primary goals are finding the notes and alternating hammers. We'll begin with the treble bridge. Strike the strings an inch or so from the bridge.

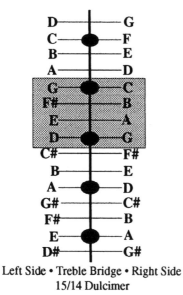

Left Side • Treble Bridge • Right Side
15/14 Dulcimer

## The G Scale

The first key (scale) to explore is G.
The notes in the G scale are
G A B C D E F# G.
Find those notes on your dulcimer, using your tuning scheme and the diagram on the left. Play the G scale all with the right hammer, then all with the left hammer, and, finally, by alternating hammers. To alternate, play G with the left hammer, A with the right, B with the left, C with the right, (cross the bridge), D with the left, E with the right, F# with the left, and end on G with the right hammer.

Here's a little tune to play. R means the right hammer; L means the left.

## First Tune • Key of G

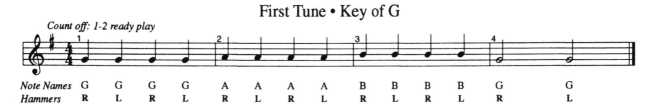

| Note Names | G | G | G | G | A | A | A | A | B | B | B | B | G | G |
|---|---|---|---|---|---|---|---|---|---|---|---|---|---|---|
| Hammers | R | L | R | L | R | L | R | L | R | L | R | L | R | L |

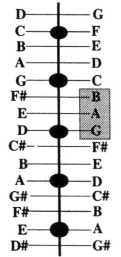

Left Side • **Treble Bridge** • Right Side
15/14 Dulcimer

The highlighted area on the diagram shows you where to find the notes for the first tune. Please note that we're using a 15/14 instrument in the diagram. If you have a smaller dulcimer, and find the diagram confusing, block off the bottom three courses. Smaller dulcimers (12/11) generally begin with the C#.

After you've played the tune using the hammering pattern written under the music, try it again, beginning with the left hammer instead of the right. Thus all of the R's are now L's, and vice versa. Although you may not feel as comfortable leading with the left hammer, the tune works just as well this way.

11

## Next Tune • Key of G

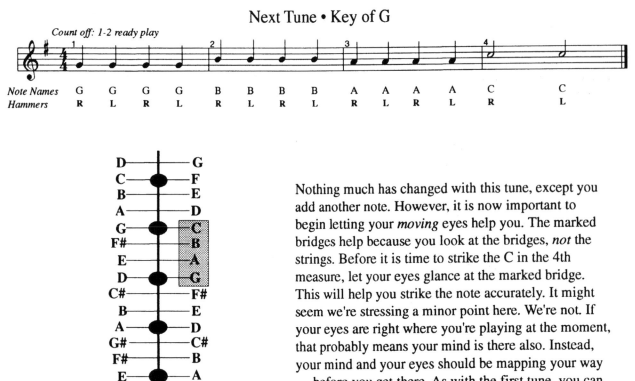

| Note Names | G | G | G | G | B | B | B | B | A | A | A | A | C | C |
|---|---|---|---|---|---|---|---|---|---|---|---|---|---|---|
| Hammers | R | L | R | L | R | L | R | L | R | L | R | L | R | L |

Left Side • **Treble Bridge** • Right Side
15/14 Dulcimer

Nothing much has changed with this tune, except you add another note. However, it is now important to begin letting your *moving* eyes help you. The marked bridges help because you look at the bridges, *not* the strings. Before it is time to strike the C in the 4th measure, let your eyes glance at the marked bridge. This will help you strike the note accurately. It might seem we're stressing a minor point here. We're not. If your eyes are right where you're playing at the moment, that probably means your mind is there also. Instead, your mind and your eyes should be mapping your way — before you get there. As with the first tune, you can play this melody reversing all of the right and left hammers.

---

## The One After That • Key of G

| Note Names | G | G | G | G | B | B | B | B | D | D | D | D | G | G |
|---|---|---|---|---|---|---|---|---|---|---|---|---|---|---|
| Hammers | L | R | L | R | L | R | L | R | L | R | L | R | L | R |

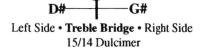

This time you lead with the left hammer instead of the right because of where you're going: to the left side of the treble bridge. When you have some facility with the tune, try reversing the right and left hammer sequence. You'll find that you have to cross your hands over the bridge. Now, we're not playing fast, and crossing hands probably won't ruin your day, but every extraneous move slows you down. In any tune, especially a fast tune, you cross hands only if that's your best playing option. Again, it is important to let your eyes lead the way. The last two notes in this tune are on the left side of a marked bridge. Let this fact register with your eyes and mind.

## Yet Another • Key of G

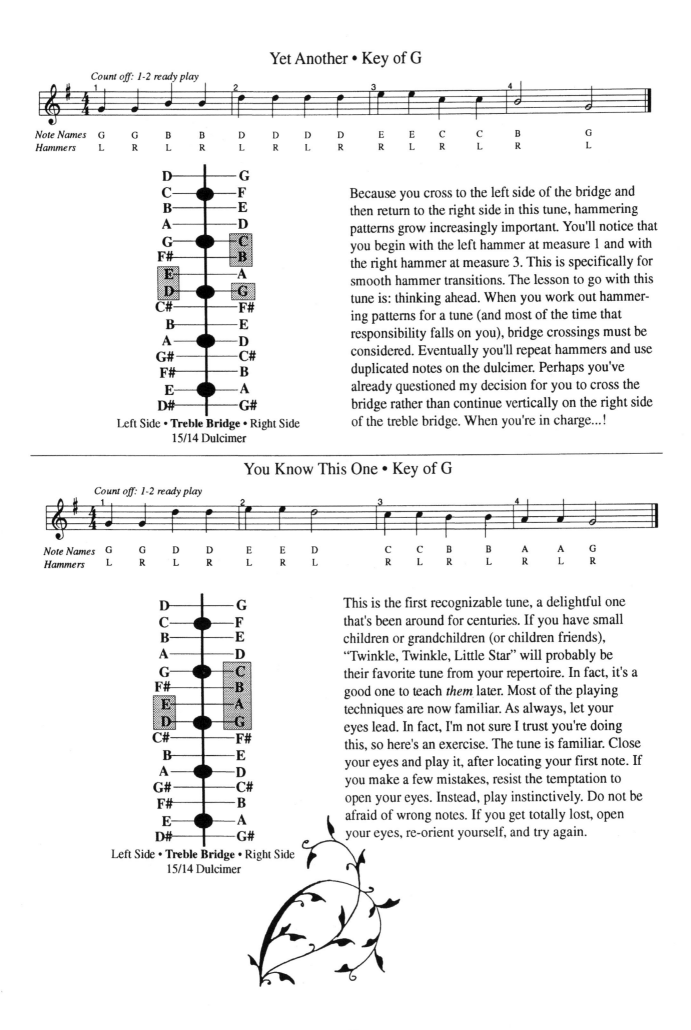

*Count off: 1-2 ready play*

| Note Names | G | G | B | B | D | D | D | D | E | E | C | C | B | G |
|------------|---|---|---|---|---|---|---|---|---|---|---|---|---|---|
| Hammers | L | R | L | R | L | R | L | R | R | L | R | L | R | L |

Left Side • **Treble Bridge** • Right Side
15/14 Dulcimer

Because you cross to the left side of the bridge and then return to the right side in this tune, hammering patterns grow increasingly important. You'll notice that you begin with the left hammer at measure 1 and with the right hammer at measure 3. This is specifically for smooth hammer transitions. The lesson to go with this tune is: thinking ahead. When you work out hammering patterns for a tune (and most of the time that responsibility falls on you), bridge crossings must be considered. Eventually you'll repeat hammers and use duplicated notes on the dulcimer. Perhaps you've already questioned my decision for you to cross the bridge rather than continue vertically on the right side of the treble bridge. When you're in charge...!

## You Know This One • Key of G

*Count off: 1-2 ready play*

| Note Names | G | G | D | D | E | E | D | C | C | B | B | A | A | G |
|------------|---|---|---|---|---|---|---|---|---|---|---|---|---|---|
| Hammers | L | R | L | R | L | R | L | R | L | R | L | R | L | R |

Left Side • **Treble Bridge** • Right Side
15/14 Dulcimer

This is the first recognizable tune, a delightful one that's been around for centuries. If you have small children or grandchildren (or children friends), "Twinkle, Twinkle, Little Star" will probably be their favorite tune from your repertoire. In fact, it's a good one to teach *them* later. Most of the playing techniques are now familiar. As always, let your eyes lead. In fact, I'm not sure I trust you're doing this, so here's an exercise. The tune is familiar. Close your eyes and play it, after locating your first note. If you make a few mistakes, resist the temptation to open your eyes. Instead, play instinctively. Do not be afraid of wrong notes. If you get totally lost, open your eyes, re-orient yourself, and try again.

## Exploring Other Keys • The Key of D

You are about to discover something interesting about the hammered dulcimer: once you learn a tune on the dulcimer in a particular key, you can transpose (move) it to another key with little effort. We're primarily talking about the keys of D and G and, on a large dulcimer, A, but there are other possibilities. Let's explore with the first five tunes you learned in the key of G. We're going to duplicate them in the key of D. Rather than present the notes on the treble bridge for each tune, I'll give you the general area once. Just so you don't have to go back and compare, all hammering patterns are the same.

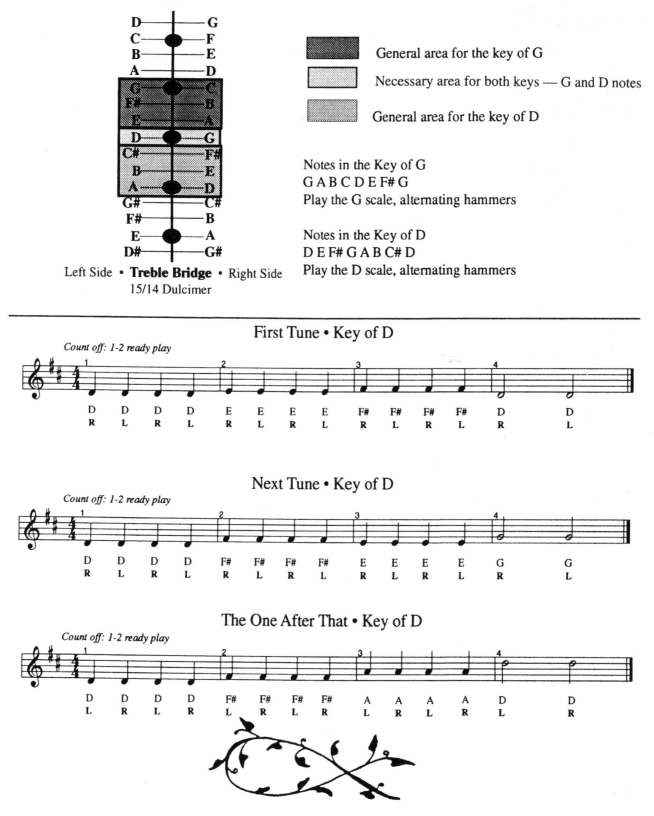

Left Side • **Treble Bridge** • Right Side
15/14 Dulcimer

General area for the key of G

Necessary area for both keys — G and D notes

General area for the key of D

Notes in the Key of G
G A B C D E F# G
Play the G scale, alternating hammers

Notes in the Key of D
D E F# G A B C# D
Play the D scale, alternating hammers

---

### First Tune • Key of D

*Count off: 1-2 ready play*

| D | D | D | D | E | E | E | E | F# | F# | F# | F# | D | D |
|---|---|---|---|---|---|---|---|----|----|----|----|---|---|
| R | L | R | L | R | L | R | L | R | L | R | L | R | L |

### Next Tune • Key of D

*Count off: 1-2 ready play*

| D | D | D | D | F# | F# | F# | F# | E | E | E | E | G | G |
|---|---|---|---|----|----|----|----|---|---|---|---|---|---|
| R | L | R | L | R | L | R | L | R | L | R | L | R | L |

### The One After That • Key of D

*Count off: 1-2 ready play*

| D | D | D | D | F# | F# | F# | F# | A | A | A | A | D | D |
|---|---|---|---|----|----|----|----|---|---|---|---|---|---|
| L | R | L | R | L | R | L | R | L | R | L | R | L | R |

14

## Yet Another • Key of D

*Count off: 1-2 ready play*

| D | D | F# | F# | A | A | A | A | B | B | G | G | F# | D |
|---|---|----|----|---|---|---|---|---|---|---|---|----|---|
| L | R | L  | R  | L | R | L | R | R | L | R | L | R  | L |

## You Know This One • Key of D

*Count off: 1-2 ready play*

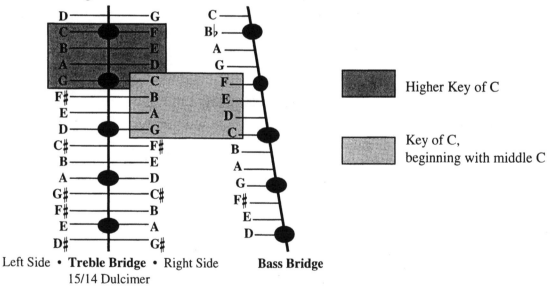

| D | D | A | A | B | B | A | G | G | F# | F# | E | E | D |
|---|---|---|---|---|---|---|---|---|----|----|---|---|---|
| L | R | L | R | L | R | L | R | L | R  | L  | R | L | R |

---

## Exploring Other Keys • Key of C

Even those who don't play piano often have a nodding acquaintance with the key of C — no sharps or flats, just the white keys — and many know how to find middle C on the piano. Other keys, like D and G and A with sharps and F with a B-flat, are the hard ones on the piano. Although the key of C, beginning with middle C, is not difficult on the hammered dulcimer, it is harder to play than the keys of G and D. The key of C involves the bass bridge, and a lot of hammered dulcimer players aren't wild about the bass bridge. However, that doesn't mean you, so here we go.

Notes in the Key of C • C D E F G A B C
Notes in the Key of G • G A B C D E F# G
The two keys use the same notes, except for F# and F.
Play both the G and C scales, alternating hammers.

Do you see the area (G, A, B, C notes) shared by the keys of C and G? This is not a rarity.
Keys share notes with each other all over the dulcimer.

15

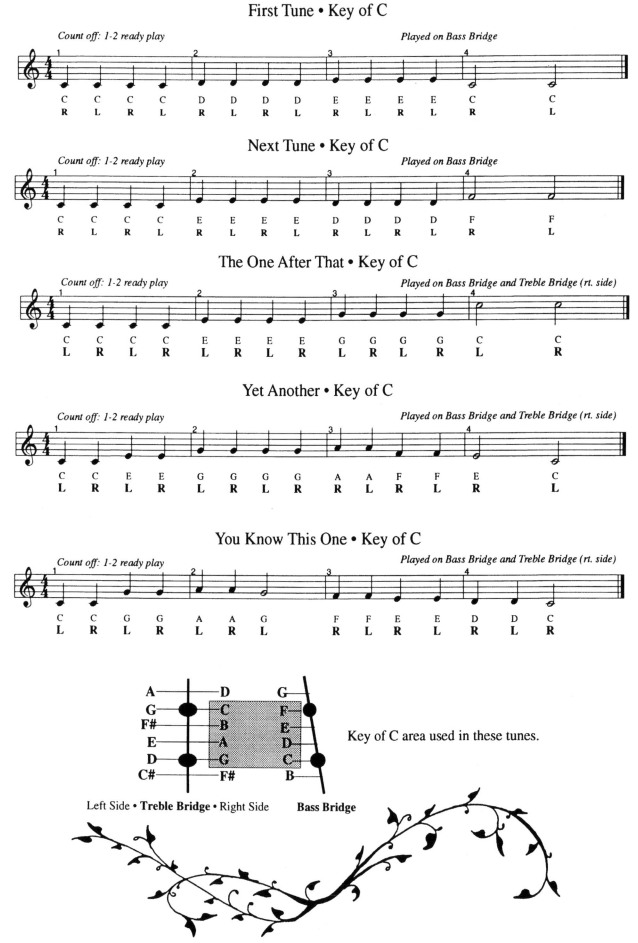

## First Tune • Key of C

*Count off: 1-2 ready play*                                          *Played on Bass Bridge*

| C | C | C | C | D | D | D | D | E | E | E | E | C | C |
| R | L | R | L | R | L | R | L | R | L | R | L | R | L |

## Next Tune • Key of C

*Count off: 1-2 ready play*                                          *Played on Bass Bridge*

| C | C | C | C | E | E | E | E | D | D | D | D | F | F |
| R | L | R | L | R | L | R | L | R | L | R | L | R | L |

## The One After That • Key of C

*Count off: 1-2 ready play*                         *Played on Bass Bridge and Treble Bridge (rt. side)*

| C | C | C | C | E | E | E | E | G | G | G | G | C | C |
| L | R | L | R | L | R | L | R | L | R | L | R | L | R |

## Yet Another • Key of C

*Count off: 1-2 ready play*                         *Played on Bass Bridge and Treble Bridge (rt. side)*

| C | C | E | E | G | G | G | G | A | A | F | F | E | C |
| L | R | L | R | L | R | L | R | R | L | R | L | R | L |

## You Know This One • Key of C

*Count off: 1-2 ready play*                         *Played on Bass Bridge and Treble Bridge (rt. side)*

| C | C | G | G | A | A | G | F | F | E | E | D | D | C |
| L | R | L | R | L | R | L | R | L | R | L | R | L | R |

Key of C area used in these tunes.

Left Side • **Treble Bridge** • Right Side          **Bass Bridge**

# Alternating Hammers

Why alternate hammers? As an experiment, strike a note in the middle of the instrument about ten times with one hammer (left or right). Observe: after awhile you begin clutching the hammer (not good for relaxation), and the sound becomes strident. Now, play the note about ten time alternating hammers (right, left, etc. or left, right, etc.). I hope you find this easier and more musical. You might notice that the left hammer sounds a little weak (if you're right-handed). This will improve as you continue to play.

Note: If you play lots of harmony notes with your melodies, you'll have to use more repeated hammers; both hammers will often be busy at the same time. Generally, tunes with a lot of harmony are played at slow or moderate speed, so this helps. Alternating hammers is not the one and only way to play the dulcimer at all times. Alternating hammers is necessary for flowing faster pieces without much harmony. In melodies with lots of harmony, alternate when you can. Your first consideration most of the time: alternating hammers.

---

# Hammering Patterns

There is often more than one hammering pattern available for a section of music. Sometimes one move is decidedly preferable over another; other times it is a matter of choice. I speak continually of horizontal moves whenever possible. Who's to say that your making a smooth vertical jump is wrong? If it works easily and well, it's all right. Duke Ellington said, "If it sounds good, it is good."

However, after playing the dulcimer for more than fifteen years, I have opinions! Some opinions are based on what I consider to be good playing habits, others are simply what works for me. I am passionate about both. To be fair, I will try to separate the two in this book. First, horizontal hammering patterns are important, especially combined with alternating hammers. Play the following hammering sequences.

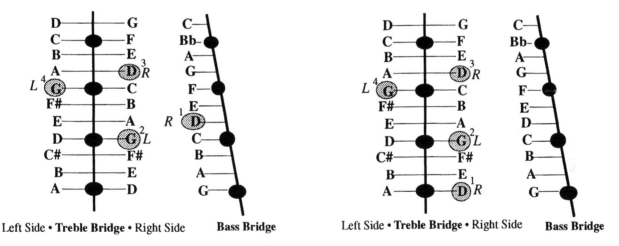

Left Side • **Treble Bridge** • Right Side      **Bass Bridge**          Left Side • **Treble Bridge** • Right Side      **Bass Bridge**

Both times you must start with the right hammer so the last note can be played with the left hammer. After you've played both sequences several times each, notice how much your eyes (and head) move on the second sequence. Are you missing more notes on that one? The first one "rolls," and almost all of the notes are in sight at the same time.

When melodic notes are separated by several tones, a horizontal move is generally preferable. You ask, "With which hammer do I begin a tune?" I ask you, "Where are you going?" Do you need the left hammer to strike a note found only on the left side of the treble bridge? Unless I or another player is lurking over your shoulder, you will be on your own most of the time. Recently I met a woman who had just stopped playing the dulcimer. "There were too many choices. I was too confused," she said.

It's a fine line. Folk music has many more playing choices than classical music. The hammered dulcimer, with two bridges and duplicated notes, means choices.

Everything is done with playing ease and fluidity in mind. Simply try to keep the music flowing.

# Are You Sleeping?

French Round

*Count Off: 1-2 Ready Play*

| | | | | | | | | | | | | | |
|---|---|---|---|---|---|---|---|---|---|---|---|---|---|
| D | E | F# | D | D | E | F# | D | F# | G | A | F# | G | A |
| L | R | L | R | L | R | L | R | L | R | L | L | R | L |

| | | | | | | | | | | | | | |
|---|---|---|---|---|---|---|---|---|---|---|---|---|---|
| A | B | A | G | F# | D | A | B | A | G | F# | D | D | A | D | D | A | D |
| L | R | L | R | L | R | L | R | L | R | L | R | L | R | L | L | R | L |

Left Side • **Treble Bridge** • Right Side
15/14 Dulcimer

You need this diagram to use the hammering directions under the note names above. There is a left hammer repeat on the F# in measure 4 and on the first D in measure 8.

Left Side • **Treble Bridge** • Right Side
15/14 Dulcimer

Here is another way to hammer "Are You Sleeping?." Because the notes run up and down the right side of the treble bridge, you can begin with either the left or right hammer. However, the first D in measure 8 must be played with the left hammer to guide you to the bass bridge for the A.

# Duplicated Notes On The Dulcimer

## Mapping Your Way Through a Tune

1. The distance between two notes is called an interval (more about them later). A large distance (interval) between two notes usually means a bridge cross (bass bridge to right side of the treble bridge or from the right side of the treble bridge to the left side).

2. Sections of melodies that "walk around" or have small intervals are usually played vertically.

3. Duplicated notes on the dulcimer help you play passages smoothly.

Here are two ways to play the following passage

| G | B | C | E | F# | G |
|---|---|---|---|----|---|
| R | L | R | L | R  | L |

Here you play totally in the key of G area. It works easily because you began playing the passage with the right hammer. However, if you begin with the left hammer, another way of playing it becomes easy:

| G | B | C | E | F# | G |
|---|---|---|---|----|---|
| L | R | L | R | L  | R |

This time you stray outside the key of G area for the E to enable a smooth transition over to the left side. Which way of playing this passage is best? Both are fine. The deciding factors are ease and smoothness of playing and as little extraneous movement as possible.

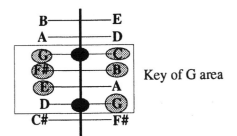

Key of G area

**Left Side • Treble Bridge • Right Side**

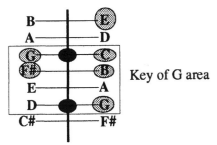

Key of G area

**Left Side • Treble Bridge • Right Side**

---

## Hammering Patterns: Melody with Harmony

Your playing should be flexible. Hammering patterns, of course, help you memorize a tune. But if you are so locked into the patterns that such and such a note can only be played with the right hammer (because you worked it out that way), it's like getting married on the first date. You're committed! If you need your right hammer for a harmony note (and it is currently in use for a melody note), switch and play the melody note with the left hammer. No questions asked. Of course, that might mean a short series of repeated left hammers. No problem.

# Mapping Your Way Through
# O Susanna

There are at least three ways to hammer this tune.

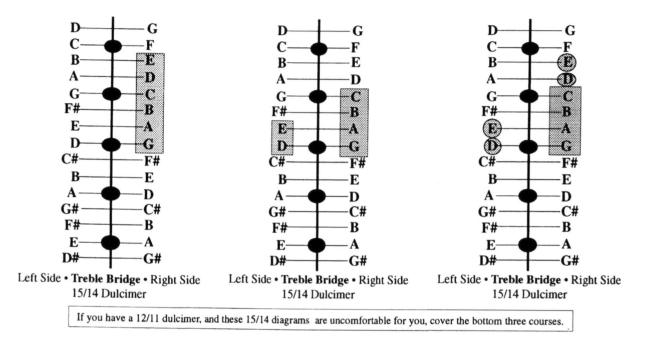

Left Side • **Treble Bridge** • Right Side
15/14 Dulcimer

Left Side • **Treble Bridge** • Right Side
15/14 Dulcimer

Left Side • **Treble Bridge** • Right Side
15/14 Dulcimer

If you have a 12/11 dulcimer, and these 15/14 diagrams are uncomfortable for you, cover the bottom three courses.

*Dulcimer Area 1:* Begin with either the left or right hammer. I suggest the right hammer. If you begin with the right hammer and alternate throughout the tune, something happens at the end of measure 12. The melody is just like the beginning, but you'll approach it with the left hammer. If it feels strange, simply repeat the right hammer.

*Dulcimer Area 2:* Begin with the right hammer for a smooth transition to the left side of the bridge (the D in measure 1). You'll need to repeat hammers for smooth transitions back and forth (measure 2, 5, 6, and so forth). Let's just say that the last strike on the left should be with the left hammer to lead to the right. The last strike on the right should be with the right hammer to lead to the left!

*Dulcimer Area 3:* The circled D's and E's are duplicated notes (the two D's are the same pitch as are the two E's). They can be used interchangeably to help with alternating hammers. This is how I'd play the tune, with occasional repeated hammers. Few of us are ambidextrous, feeling more comfortable leading off a section with either our right or left hands. Flexibility can help us play with ease.

20

# O Susanna

Stephen Foster

*Count Off: 1 Ready Play*

♩ = *132*

G A B D D    E D B G    G A B  B A G    A        G A

B D D    E D B G    G A B  B A A G    G A B

C  C    E E    E D D B G    A        G A

B D D    E D B G    G A B  B A A G    B G

*Soundholes are signatures of the builders. I can look at a soundhole and often know who built the dulcimer.*

# Exploring Four Keys

## Go Tell Aunt Rhody • Key of G

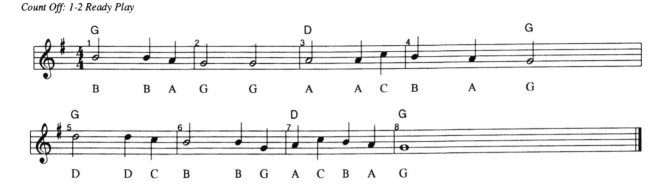

This old American tune has five notes in it. In the key of G, those are G A B C and D. Locate the key of G area on your dulcimer and try the tune. If you begin with your right hammer and alternate, you will be in position to play the two Ds in measure 5 on the left side of the treble bridge, repeating the left hammer. That D is also duplicated so you can play it on the right side of the treble bridge (boxed in on the diagram). Your choice.

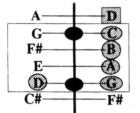

Left Side • **Treble Bridge** • Right Side
Isolated Key of G area

## Go Tell Aunt Rhody • Key of D

Left Side • **Treble Bridge** • Right Side
Isolated Key of D area

Locate the key of D area on the dulcimer. Notice that little has changed from the key of G area; you've simply moved down three courses. The instructions for playing "Go Tell Aunt Rhody" in the key of D are the same as those for the key of G.

## Go Tell Aunt Rhody • Key of C

*Count Off: 1-2 Ready Play*

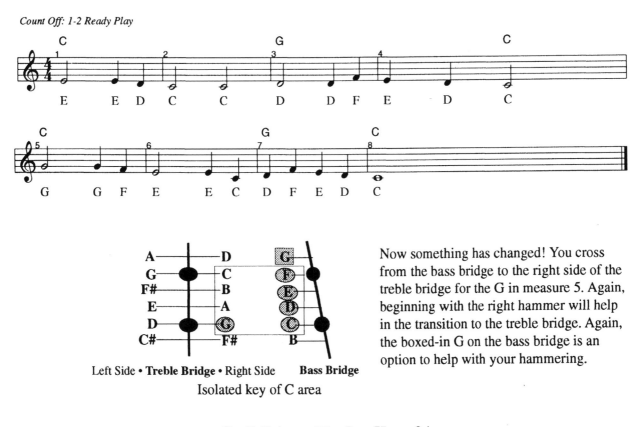

Now something has changed! You cross from the bass bridge to the right side of the treble bridge for the G in measure 5. Again, beginning with the right hammer will help in the transition to the treble bridge. Again, the boxed-in G on the bass bridge is an option to help with your hammering.

Left Side • **Treble Bridge** • Right Side　　**Bass Bridge**
Isolated key of C area

## Go Tell Aunt Rhody • Key of A

*Count Off: 1-2 ready play*

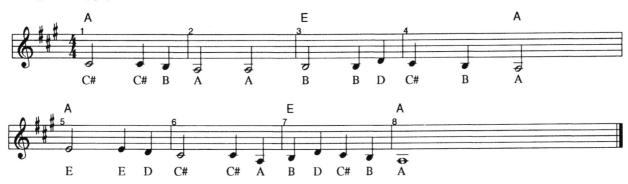

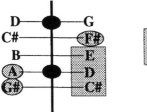 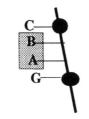

Left Side • **Treble Bridge** • Right Side　　**Bass Bridge**
Isolated area for playing the tune in the key of A

If you have a 15/14 dulcimer, the key of A can be found on the treble bridge beginning three courses under the key of D. Just for the practice, however, try playing the key of A as we have it on the diagram. Notes in the key of A are A B C# D E F# G# A. Try playing the key of A scale. The additional notes needed for the scale are circled.

23

# Hammering Exercises in the Key of G

Beginning with these exercises, suggested hammering patterns throughout the book are indicated with the following shapes:

◇ Bass bridge
□ Right side treble bridge
○ Left side treble bridge

24

# Hammering Exercises in the Key of D

25

# Learning Scales and String Courses

I assume your purpose in learning to play the instrument is not to add angst to your life. Instead, you're playing the dulcimer, I'm sure, to add enjoyment and creativity to your life while interacting with other musicians. If you can pick out tunes, why learn what notes you're playing on the dulcimer? Because I agree with your presumed reasons, it's difficult for me to say some discipline is helpful and even necessary.

Perhaps you ask a guitarist friend to play a tune with you. When s/he inquires, "What key?," "I have no idea" is not the best answer. If, instead, you say, "Let's see, it hangs around in the middle of the dulcimer. It has F#s, but not C#s. It ends on G, I think it's in the key of G." Then you've used growing musical knowledge plus an understanding of the instrument to be a real participant in the music process. As a bonus, knowing what you're playing on the instrument will help you read written music. Try the following Gain-But-No-Pain method of learning the names of the string courses (hereafter called notes) on the dulcimer.

First, keep the instrument where it is accessible. A dulcimer in its case takes time to set up and play. Choose a key to explore for awhile. In this example, we'll use the key of D.

The notes in the D scale are D E F# G A B C# D. Find the area where the key of D lies on the treble bridge of your dulcimer.

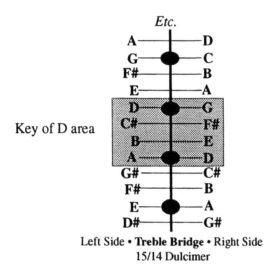

Key of D area

Left Side • **Treble Bridge** • Right Side
15/14 Dulcimer

Play D on the right side of the treble bridge.

The octave D (higher) is on the left side of the treble bridge. Play it.

Look at the two D's. What characteristics of the string courses can help you find the notes quickly? One D is on the right side of a marked course; the other is on the left side of a marked course. This can help.

*Good exercise for letting your eyes roam around the instrument as you play:* Play the right-side D. Look at the left-side D, then play it. Look back at the right-side D and play it.

---

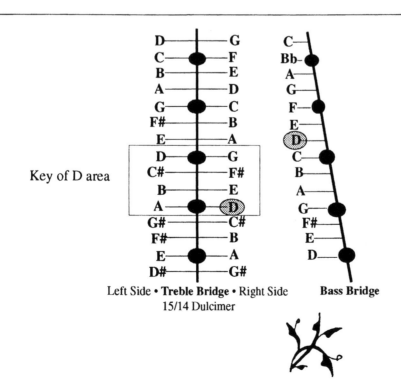

Key of D area

Left Side • **Treble Bridge** • Right Side          **Bass Bridge**
15/14 Dulcimer

On the bass bridge there is a D with the same pitch as the right-side treble bridge D. Find it, either by sound or by the tuning scheme sheet that came with your dulcimer.

How can you find it quickly? It is just above a marked course (C), about in the middle of the instrument. It is also, typically, the 5th or 8th course from the bottom, but counting courses when playing slows you down!

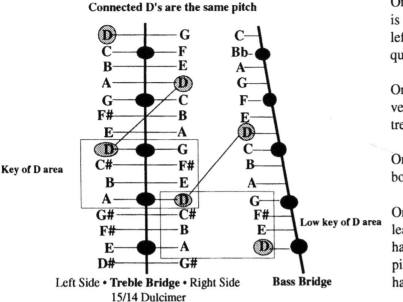

**Connected D's are the same pitch**

Key of D area

Low key of D area

Left Side • **Treble Bridge** • Right Side
15/14 Dulcimer

Bass Bridge

On the right side of the treble bridge there is a D with the same pitch as the D on the left side of the bridge. How can you find it quickly?

On most dulcimers there is a high D at or very near the top of the left side of the treble bridge.

On a 15/14 dulcimer there's a low D at the bottom of the bass bridge.

On a 15/14 dulcimer there are six D's at least. On a 12/11 dulcimer you probably have five. Some of the D's are the same pitch and, therefore, will help you with hammering patterns.

Play all of the D's on your dulcimer, finding them as quickly as you can (eyes before hammers). Compare and contrast the low or high pitches. Work on learning the placement of the Ds on your instrument until you can strike them all with little thought. The easiest way to do this is to stop for a minute or so to find them each time you pass the instrument. *Just a reminder: While learning notes on the instrument, you, I hope, are still playing and learning tunes just for the fun of it.*

# Learning More Notes in the Key Of D

Review the notes in the D scale: D E F# G A B C# D

It seems logical that you'd now work on learning the placement of E's since you know where the D's are. Not necessarily. Now is the time to learn a bit of music theory that will help you in all of your music playing. Mathematicians and scientists have worked for centuries organizing sound. Music theory and acoustics books delve into this fascinating subject, and I suggest you investigate further if you're interested. For now, I'll just introduce a few theoretical items that apply to your hammered dulcimer playing.

The distance between D and A is called a 5th interval. If you count the notes in the scale from D to A you'll find five. The 5th is a very important interval. It is way more important than the interval between D and E (a 2nd), for example. When you strike a note, other notes, called harmonics, sing along. This occurs not only on the dulcimer but on other instruments, with your voice, and in various things around us that produce sound. In music, the first harmonics to be "excited" by a struck note are the 5th, 4th, and octave. Our ears can hear these intervals better than, say, a 2nd because harmonics reinforce them. Harmony centuries ago was filled with 5ths, 4ths and octaves because they just felt "right." Later when we play chords we'll mainly use those built on the 1st, 4th, and 5th scale tones of whatever key we're in.

You play a 5th interval instrument. The distance across the treble bridge is a 5th. Right away you can hear the 5th in your mind if you think of the second twinkle in "Twinkle, Twinkle, Little Star." Play the D on the right side of the treble bridge and then the A directly across from it. The A is our next note to learn, followed by G, the 4th tone in the D scale.

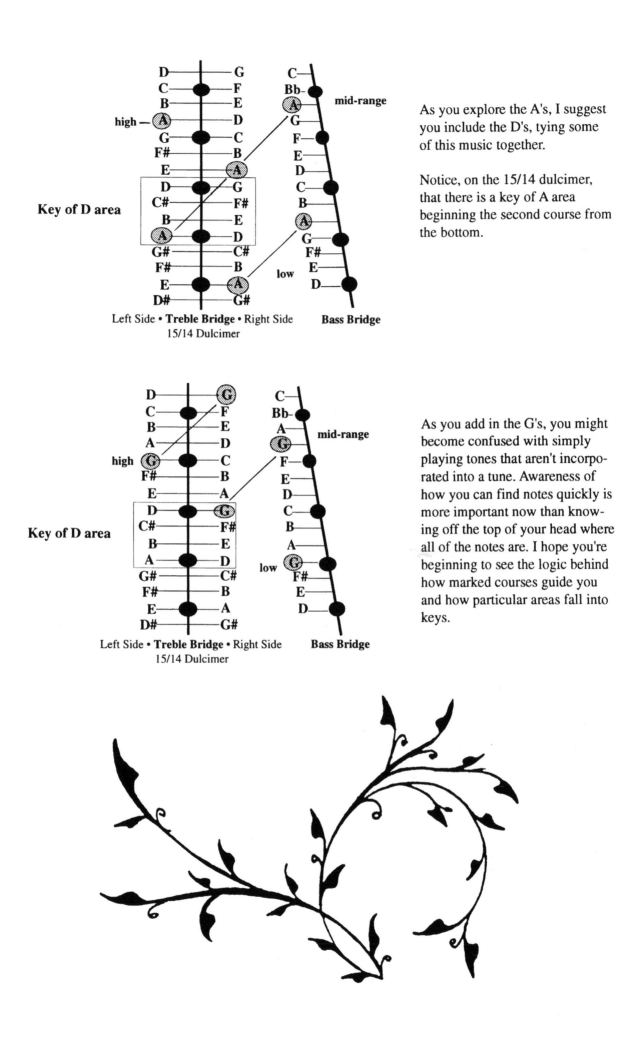

**Key of D area**

Left Side • **Treble Bridge** • Right Side
15/14 Dulcimer

**Bass Bridge**

As you explore the A's, I suggest you include the D's, tying some of this music together.

Notice, on the 15/14 dulcimer, that there is a key of A area beginning the second course from the bottom.

**Key of D area**

Left Side • **Treble Bridge** • Right Side
15/14 Dulcimer

**Bass Bridge**

As you add in the G's, you might become confused with simply playing tones that aren't incorporated into a tune. Awareness of how you can find notes quickly is more important now than knowing off the top of your head where all of the notes are. I hope you're beginning to see the logic behind how marked courses guide you and how particular areas fall into keys.

28

Next are the interior notes of the D scale — E F# B and C# — where you'll notice something. None of these notes is on a marked bridge. Also notice there is no C# on the bass bridge.

Here's a good way to learn the locations of the E F# B and C#. Place your hammer (without striking) on the D, right side of the treble bridge (the marked course). Look at E, one course higher. Strike E. Go back to D. Look at F#, then strike it. Back to D. Look at G, then strike it. Back to D. Continue up to the octave D (left side).

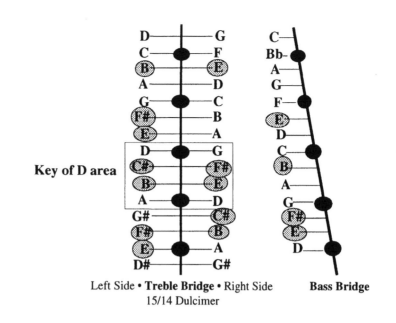

**Key of D area**

Left Side • **Treble Bridge** • Right Side
15/14 Dulcimer

**Bass Bridge**

You can make this exercise harder in various ways. Start at D in the key of D area. Look at E (above that D), then strike. Find another E, same pitch, on the bass bridge, then strike. If you have a 15/14 dulcimer, there is another E of the same pitch on the left side of the treble bridge near the bottom. Now find the octave higher and lower (if any) E's. Do the same with the F#s and so forth.

You can also mix up the notes in the D scale. Beginning with D, look for and strike random notes such as B followed by F#.

Don't say, "Huh?" just yet. Find a marked course (bass or treble) and play an ascending scale. The notes go up four courses, over (to the right side treble bridge or to the left side treble bridge) and up four courses. See how all of the keys mingle with each other, sharing some important 4th and 5th notes of the scale. Find the lowest G on the bass bridge. The low G scale begins there. Follow it up four courses, over to the treble bridge and up four courses. By doing that, you'll find a needed F# is on the treble bridge, not the bass bridge.

The following scales are outlined on this diagram:

D • D E F# G A B C# D
G • G A B C D E F# G
C • C D E F G A B C
F • F G A B-flat C D E F
A • A B C# D E F# G# A (15/14 inst.)

Study the diagram for a while. Follow the scales with your eyes and then play them on your dulcimer.

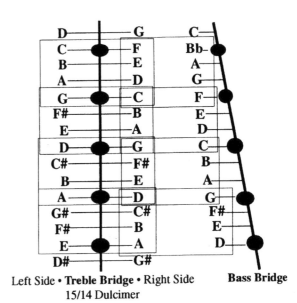

Left Side • **Treble Bridge** • Right Side · **Bass Bridge**
15/14 Dulcimer

Here's a little note/scale learning exercise for you. Find the low A on the bass bridge. You know (from the key of A on the treble bridge in the diagram) that notes in the key of A are A B C# D E F# G# A. With your eyes, run an A scale beginning with that bass bridge A. See how you need the bass bridge and both sides of the treble bridge to get all of the notes? The brave among you can try this one. Find E (the low one) on the bass bridge. The notes in the key of E are E F# G# A B C# D# E. Run the scale, knowing you'll need the bass and treble bridges. Want to try the key of B? The notes are B C# D# E F# G# A# B. You can do it; Bb and A# are the same note, by the way. Most things are possible on the dulcimer; some are not easy!

# Practice Tune
# Golden Slippers

"Golden Slippers" is a staple at old-time music jams. I like to fill in some notes that are long in value (perhaps lasting three beats) by such methods as found in measure 29. Think up your own, fun ways to "mark time."

This tune has few notes and lots of similar phrases. For example, measures 5 and 6 are the same as measures 1 and 2, one course lower. Measure 1 starts with a D; measure 5 with a C#. This might help you in learning and playing it.

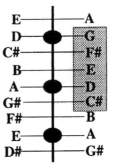 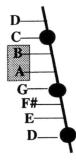

Left Side • **Treble Bridge** • Right Side · **Bass Bridge**
15/14 Dulcimer

# Golden Slippers

Traditional American Tune

31

# Duplicated Notes and Repeated Hammers
# Home on the Range

"Home on the Range" presents you with choices; which duplicated note to use (in this case, D and E); and when to repeat hammers. The second question is tied into the first, for the hammer you use brings you closer (vertically or horizontally) to which note to use.

Repeat the right hammer on the first two notes of the tune. This will easily bring the left hammer into place for the G in measure 1.

When you map out a tune on the dulcimer, work out the most important jumps and running patterns first. In measure 3, if you use the treble bridge E, you have a long vertical jump to the C, also in that measure. I prefer to use the bass bridge E. To do that easily, you should play the F# prior to that (end of measure 2) with your left hammer. Which means, the G prior to the F# should be played with the right hammer! Knowing where you need to end up often helps you decide where to start.

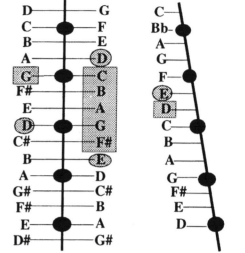

Left Side • **Treble Bridge** • Right Side
15/14 Dulcimer

**Bass Bridge**

# Home On The Range

Cowboy Song

◇  Bass bridge
☐  Right side treble bridge
◯  Left side treble bridge

# More Hammering Patterns
# Arkansas Traveler

Whenever more than one bridge is involved, you'll surely have repeated hammers. To keep repeated hammers to a minimum, take advantage of duplicated notes (A on both the right side and left side of the treble bridge, for example. They are circled on the diagram.) Opt for horizontal moves when possible.

Look at measures 6 and 7. A large jump almost always means a horizontal move. In this case, however, there are two large jumps, one after the other. One jump must be vertical. Try D to A (measure 6) as a vertical move, followed by a horizontal move to the first D in measure 7.

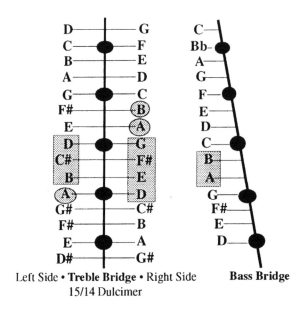

Left Side • **Treble Bridge** • Right Side
15/14 Dulcimer

**Bass Bridge**

"The Arkansas Traveler" moves quickly. If a hammer pattern of yours doesn't seem to fit the tempo, change the pattern! Make the tune dance. Without a nice dancing feel, this tune is just a bunch of notes.

# Arkansas Traveler

*Count Off: 1 Ready Play*

American Tune

*More hammering patterns*

◇ Bass bridge
▢ Right side treble bridge
○ Left side treble bridge

35

# Vertical and Horizontal Moves, Repeat Signs
# Liberty

This wonderful tune is prefect for practicing vertical and horizontal moves — and for deciding which to do when! "Liberty," at hoedown speed, moves quickly, so good hammering patterns are a must. Look at measure 1 — it begins with F#. The third note is an A. You have two A's of that pitch on the treble bridge, one on the right side, the other on the left. If you do not immediately see why you should play the A on the right side, try the move from the F# to both A's for a while. That should convince you!

In figuring out your hammering pattern, consider the jump to the right side. The note prior to the jump should be played with the left hammer for a smooth move. Does this mean that the first note in measure 1 — the F# — should be played with the right hammer? In theory, yes. But, I prefer that you use two left hammers at the beginning of measure 1 so your right hammer will be in place for the A.

Figuring out hammering patterns can bog you down if you continually worry about alternating. Suppose we say that the note prior to a bridge cross should be played with whichever hammer to keep you from crossing hands. Other than that, as long as you're *mainly* alternating hammers, you're all right. This takes off a little of the pressure to be perfect.

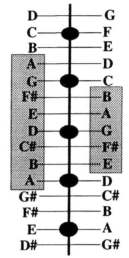

Left Side • Treble Bridge • Right Side
15/14 Dulcimer

Notes in measures 2, 4, 6, 7, and others "walk around." Any jumps are very small and the melody returns quickly to notes found only on one side of the bridge. Play these sections vertically.

Measure 10 has a decision for you. From B to D is a small jump. This is one of those situations where either a vertical or horizontal move works.

**Repeat Signs:** Those of you who read music are familiar with repeat signs, but I want to mention them for anyone who needs to know. When you get to the end of measure 8 in "Liberty," you see dots to the left of the vertical lines. The vertical lines are called bar lines, by the way. Go back either to the beginning or until you find dots on the right side of a bar line. In this tune you return to the beginning. Repeat the first eight measures and then continue. At the end of measure 16, there are dots again. As you go back, you find dots on the right side of the bar line at the beginning of the pick-up to measure 9. Repeat from there through measure 16.

# Liberty

Count Off: 1 Ready Play

Traditional Southern Tune

◇ Bass bridge
▢ Right side treble bridge
◯ Left side treble bridge

# Hornpipes, Transitional Notes, and Another Repeat
# Harvest Home

**The Hornpipe:** A hornpipe can be notated with groups of dotted eighth notes followed by sixteenth notes or by groups of two eighth notes.

Eighth note groups        Dotted eighth and sixteenth note groups

Because eighth and sixteenth note groups make the tune appear more difficult than it is, I've used eighth note groups with it. "Off to California," later in the book, is also a hornpipe and is notated the same way. Think of the rhythmic feel of a hornpipe as walking with one foot on the curb, the other in the gutter — DAH-dah, DAH-dah (long-short, long-short).

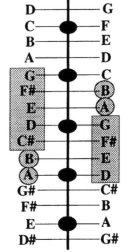

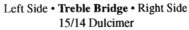

Left Side • **Treble Bridge** • Right Side
15/14 Dulcimer

**Transitional Notes:** Doubtless you've noticed that your dulcimer's duplicated notes help you get around faster. We can also call them transitional notes. I've marked two A's and two B's with circles on the diagram. Suppose you're heading up the scale from G on the right to D on the left — G A B C# D. There is only one G of that pitch on the treble bridge in that area; it's on the right. There is only one C# of that pitch; it's on the left. Both A and B are duplicated on each side of the treble bridge. To keep your hammers alternating nicely, you can cross the bridge either on the A *or* the B. Measure 12 contains a run down from E on the left to D (first note in measure 13) on the right. If you start the measure with a left hammer, you move to the right side on G. If you begin with the right hammer, you can smoothly cross to the right side on A.

**Repeat Signs — A Review:** When you get to the end of measure 8 in "Harvest Home," you see dots to the left of the bar lines. Go back to the beginning and repeat the first eight measures. At the end of measure 16, there are dots again. Repeat measures 9 through 16.

**Playing Suggestion:** I prefer playing measure 1 of "Harvest Home" all on the right side of the treble bridge (rather than playing the note A on the left). That vertical move feels comfortable. There are a lot of occasions for horizontal playing; measures 3, 9, and 11 are among them.

# Harvest Home

Count Off: 1 Ready Play

Irish Hornpipe

♩ = 120

**D**

1
A D A F# A D A F# A D E F# E D C# B A

**A7**

2
E A F# A G A F# A

3

**Emin** **A** **D**

4 E D C# B A G F# E 5 D A F# A D A F# A 6 D E F# E D C# B A

**A7** **D**

7 E A F# A G E C# E D F# D

**A7**

8 C# D E A A A F# A A A

9

**Emin** **A**

10 G A F# A E A A A 11 E A F# A G A F# A 12 E D C# B A G F# E

**D** **A7** **D**

13 D A F# A D A F# A 14 D E F# E D C# B A 15 E A F# A G E C# E 16 D F# D

◇ Bass bridge
□ Right side treble bridge
○ Left side treble bridge

# A Useful Note on the Bass Bridge
# Annie Laurie

*Many* players ignore the middle section of the bass bridge. *Most* players ignore the top of the bass bridge, except when a B♭ is needed.

Look at measure 9. The notes are C and D, leading to an E in measure 10. All of those notes should be played on the right side of the treble bridge. Continuing in measure 10, you have a G leading to a C in measure 11. See how close the G on the bass bridge is to both the E (the note before G in measure 10) and to the C (the note after G, in measure 11)?

Consulting the diagram, you'll find that all of this tune can be played easily on the bass bridge and the right side of the treble bridge. Playing in the key of C might feel strange as most of your work has been with the treble bridge. However, this lovely tune sounds nice in the key of C. I suggest you return to "Annie Laurie" after you've played chords and interval harmony. Try some harmony in this tune.

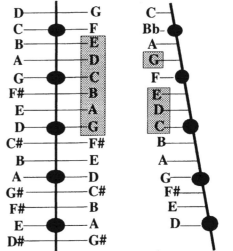

Left Side • **Treble Bridge** • Right Side
15/14 Dulcimer  **Bass Bridge**

40

# Annie Laurie

Traditional English

◇  Bass bridge
▢  Right side treble bridge
◯  Left side treble bridge

41

# Practice Tune
# No Place Like Home

There are two effective ways to play this lovely waltz depending on your starting hammer. Both work! If you begin the pickup to measure 1 with your right hammer, you move smoothly over to the left side of the treble bridge for the D at the beginning of measure two 2. If you begin with your left hammer, it is easy to play the D (measure 2) vertically on the right side of the treble bridge. The G on the bass bridge is right there to help with a horizontal move (the B to G in measure 2).

Most of measures 9 through 16 is played on the left side of the treble bridge. However, the C you need several times is on the right side of the bridge only. You might use the D just above that C to transition nicely back to the left side of the bridge (last note of measure 12 leading to the G in measure 13).

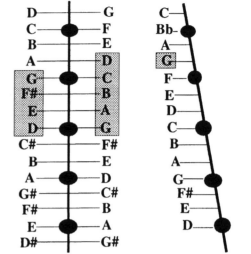

Left Side • **Treble Bridge** • Right Side
15/14 Dulcimer

**Bass Bridge**

42

# No Place Like Home

*Count Off: 1 Play*

English Waltz

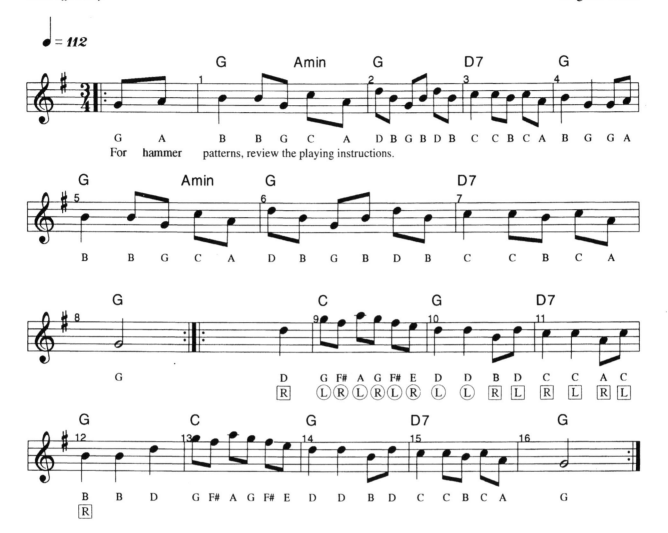

For hammer patterns, review the playing instructions.

◇ Bass bridge
☐ Right side treble bridge
◯ Left side treble bridge

43

# Intervals

The distance between two notes is called an interval. It's easy to call them chords, but a chord must have three or more notes. Intervals have two. The intervals with which we'll work are part of scales; no odd notes. We'll begin with the key of G. The notes in a G scale are G A B D E F# G. The interval between G and A is a 2nd. The others are: G to B, a 3rd; G to C, a 4th; G to D a 5th, G to E a 6th and G to F# a 7th. Most intervals are major or minor. G to B is a major third; E to G is a minor third. The first two notes of "The Marine's Hymn" are a major third; the first two notes of "Greensleeves" are a minor third. But, what makes the difference is a subject all in itself, and one left for another day. More on minors on page 66.

We're going to study intervals as a way to help you read music faster on the dulcimer (especially music with harmony notes). The appearance of the most commonly used intervals is distinctive and quickly recognizable. When you learn which intervals are typically played vertically or horizontally, decisions concerning hammering patterns are much easier. Should you wish to delve into the makeup of intervals (more than we discuss in the section on chords), a music theory book can help you.

## Intervals • 2nds

Some of us really like the tension of the 2nd intervals. They're often used with notes that are repeated. For example, if you're harmonizing two B's, the first harmony note can be an A (2nd interval) while the next harmony note is a G (a 3rd interval). Moving from a 2nd to a 3rd, for example, is called a resolution. You have taken the tension (the 2nd) and sweetened it (the 3rd). Try the sequences below and see what you think. Second intervals should be played vertically, if both notes you need are on the same bridge.

A/G    D/C    B/A    B/G

## Intervals • 3rds

You might call 3rds "sweet intervals." They decorate airs, harp tunes, waltzes, and songs just beautifully when used in moderation. In fact, all of the harmony tools we're discussing in this section are best when not overused; they then stand out better.

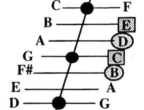

You can play the two Thirds this way (recommended).

In adapting written music to the dulcimer, your eyes can eventually tell you what you're playing (and probably where to play it) just by the shape of the intervals. When you see

D/B    E/C

...think "two courses apart (if vertical), and play vertically if possible." Isn't that what you thought?

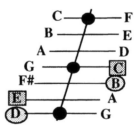

Or, this way, using duplicated notes on the left side.

In the example above, you had an option of playing the 3rds vertically or horizontally. In the following example, you have a long stretch of 3rds, and vertical is the way to go. Play measures 1 and 2 on the left side and change to the right side for measures 3 and 4. The diagrams above will help you find the notes. Practice playing the 3rds slow and fast, up and back. Aren't they pretty?

B/G    A/F#    G/E    F#/D    E/C    D/B    C/A    B/G

## Intervals • 4ths

4ths are close enough together that they can be played vertically with ease; yet, if you need to cross the bridge for melody notes, they work equally well horizontally, Melodically, the 4th interval is at the beginning of many tunes ("Amazing Grace," for example). In a melody, I generally suggest that you play a 4th interval horizontally; in harmony (a melody note with a harmony note that together make a 4th interval), it is your decision (vertical or horizontal).

A/E     C/G     E/B     G/D

## Intervals • 5ths

You play a fifth interval dulcimer. The easiest way for you to hear a 5th is to play any note on the right side of the treble bridge (disregarding any offset bridges at the very top) followed by the note directly across from it on the left side of the treble bridge. You can also go from the bass bridge to the right side of the treble bridge horizontally. D on the bass to A on the treble is an example. 5ths provide an open harmony. Centuries ago when harmony was first used, the 5th was considered appropriate and proper! I love 5th intervals and use them liberally. Play them horizontally, crossing bridges.

D/G     A/D     D/G     G/C

## Intervals • 6ths

6th intervals are also very sweet, for a reason. A 3rd interval is B and G (top to bottom). The corresponding 6th interval is G and B (top to bottom). 3rds and 6ths are powerful harmonic arranging tools. They are played horizontally, crossing bridges. Play the example below on the bass bridge and the right side of the treble bridge.

G/B     A/C     B/D     C/E

## Intervals • 7ths

Of all the harmonic intervals we've discussed, the 7th will probably be your least favorite. The example is G on the right side of the treble bridge with F# on the left side of the treble bridge. 7ths, of course, are played horizontally across bridges. Fill in the middle with some notes and you have what we call a G major7 chord. Play G and B on the right side of the bridge followed by D and F# on the left side of the bridge. (If you start with the right hammer, you can play the D on the right.) Major7 chords are wonderful and jazzy. Use F (an out-of-key note) instead of the F# and you have a G7 chord which is frequently used in the key of D.

G/F#     G/B/D/F#     G/F     G/B/D/F

## Intervals • 8ths (Octaves)

The octave is simply a note duplicated higher or lower. Octaves make especially nice endings. Play them horizontally.

G/G     A/A     D/D     G/G

# Intervals • Exercises

The four following harmony interval exercises vary in playing area and in complexity. I believe you'll find the exercises in the key of G and C, which fall mainly on the treble bridge, easier than those in D and A, which use the bass bridge a lot. I suggest you look at the exercises first (covering up the "answers" if you can) to get the various shapes in your mind. Next, visualize vertical and horizontal playing patterns. To review:

2nds • almost always vertical.
3rds • generally vertical, although your hammering pattern might require some horizontal playing.
4ths • horizontal or vertical according to your hammering patterns.
5ths • horizontal.
6ths • horizontal.
7ths • horizontal.
Octaves • horizontal.

The exercises, although in different keys, are mainly alike. I changed a few of the intervals to fit dulcimer ranges. Again, try to visualize the position of the intervals on the dulcimer before actually playing them. After you finish, go back and try to play the intervals as separate notes. For example, in the key of G, play G, followed by the low G, followed by G, then D and so forth. This will acquaint you with the intervals as harmony *and* melody. Diagrams throughout the book will help you find the notes.

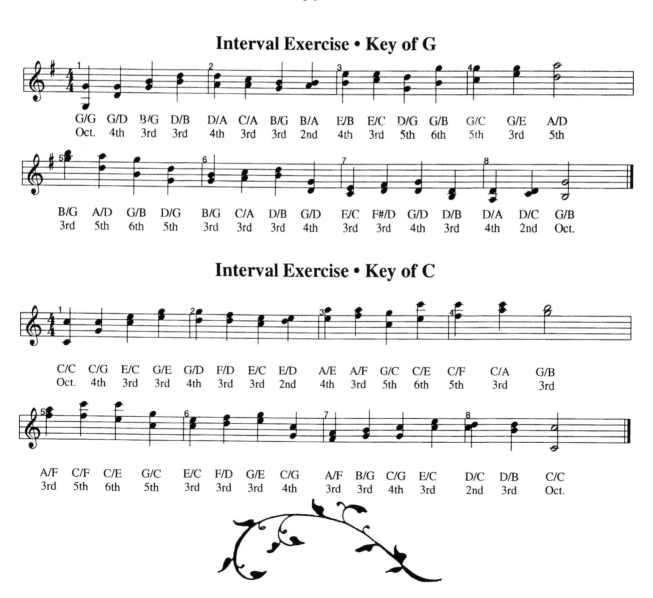

## Interval Exercise • Key of G

| G/G | G/D | B/G | D/B | D/A | C/A | B/G | B/A | E/B | E/C | D/G | G/B | G/C | G/E | A/D |
| Oct. | 4th | 3rd | 3rd | 4th | 3rd | 3rd | 2nd | 4th | 3rd | 5th | 6th | 5th | 3rd | 5th |

| B/G | A/D | G/B | D/G | B/G | C/A | D/B | G/D | E/C | F#/D | G/D | D/B | D/A | D/C | G/B |
| 3rd | 5th | 6th | 5th | 3rd | 3rd | 3rd | 4th | 3rd | 3rd | 4th | 3rd | 4th | 2nd | Oct. |

## Interval Exercise • Key of C

| C/C | C/G | E/C | G/E | G/D | F/D | E/C | E/D | A/E | A/F | G/C | C/E | C/F | C/A | G/B |
| Oct. | 4th | 3rd | 3rd | 4th | 3rd | 3rd | 2nd | 4th | 3rd | 5th | 6th | 5th | 3rd | 3rd |

| A/F | C/F | C/E | G/C | E/C | F/D | G/E | C/G | A/F | B/G | C/G | E/C | D/C | D/B | C/C |
| 3rd | 5th | 6th | 5th | 3rd | 3rd | 3rd | 4th | 3rd | 3rd | 4th | 3rd | 2nd | 3rd | Oct. |

# Interval Exercise • Key of D

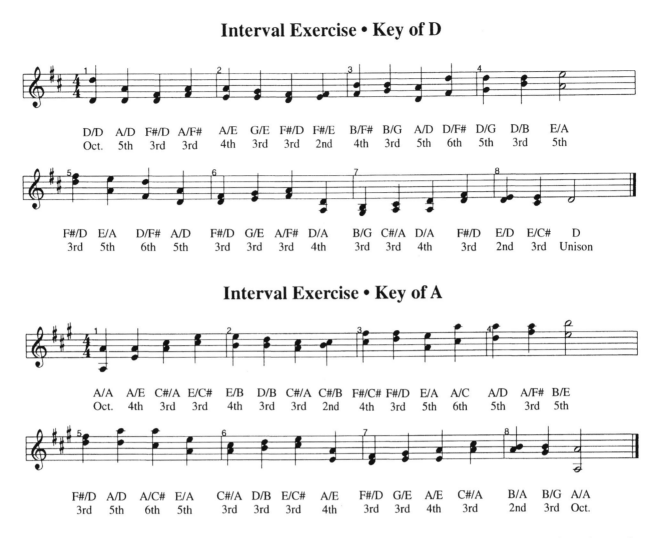

| D/D | A/D | F#/D | A/F# | A/E | G/E | F#/D | F#/E | B/F# | B/G | A/D | D/F# | D/G | D/B | E/A |
|-----|-----|------|------|-----|-----|------|------|------|-----|-----|------|-----|-----|-----|
| Oct. | 5th | 3rd | 3rd | 4th | 3rd | 3rd | 2nd | 4th | 3rd | 5th | 6th | 5th | 3rd | 5th |

| F#/D | E/A | D/F# | A/D | F#/D | G/E | A/F# | D/A | B/G | C#/A | D/A | F#/D | E/D | E/C# | D |
|------|-----|------|-----|------|-----|------|-----|-----|------|-----|------|-----|------|---|
| 3rd | 5th | 6th | 5th | 3rd | 3rd | 3rd | 4th | 3rd | 3rd | 4th | 3rd | 2nd | 3rd | Unison |

# Interval Exercise • Key of A

| A/A | A/E | C#/A | E/C# | E/B | D/B | C#/A | C#/B | F#/C# | F#/D | E/A | A/C | A/D | A/F# | B/E |
|-----|-----|------|------|-----|-----|------|------|-------|------|-----|-----|-----|------|-----|
| Oct. | 4th | 3rd | 3rd | 4th | 3rd | 3rd | 2nd | 4th | 3rd | 5th | 6th | 5th | 3rd | 5th |

| F#/D | A/D | A/C# | E/A | C#/A | D/B | E/C# | A/E | F#/D | G/E | A/E | C#/A | B/A | B/G | A/A |
|------|-----|------|-----|------|-----|------|-----|------|-----|-----|------|-----|-----|-----|
| 3rd | 5th | 6th | 5th | 3rd | 3rd | 3rd | 4th | 3rd | 3rd | 4th | 3rd | 2nd | 3rd | Oct. |

Because you need a C# and G# that are only on the left side of the treble bridge, you'll need to play a lot on the left side. Also, because several of the notes aren't duplicated, the horizontal/vertical guidelines won't always work.

47

# Playing a Tune Using Interval Harmonies
# Deck The Halls

First, look at "Deck The Halls." Try to determine, at a glance, whether the intervals are 3rds, 4ths, or 5ths (or something else, like an octave). When you can do this quickly, hammering patterns will often fall more easily into place.

5ths are almost always horizontal. Here's a 5th that fits into the tiny place left by "almost always." Look at measure 9, the C and F#. Actually, this interval isn't a 5th; it's a little smaller than that. But it looks like a 5th, and hammer-wise would generally follow the rules. You have only one C and F# of those pitches on the treble bridge. It is, therefore, played vertically.

In measure 15, play all of the 3rds vertically.

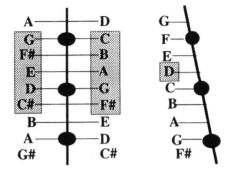

Left Side • **Treble Bridge** • Right Side    **Bass Bridge**

In a little while, you'll study modulations. Come back to "Deck The Halls" then and study the modulation from the key of G to the key of D in measures 11 and 12.

# Deck The Halls

Welsh Carol

*Count Off: 1-2 Ready Play*

# Chords

The hammered dulcimer is usually considered a melody instrument. However, being able to use it to back up other instruments has at least three advantages:

1. The musical experience in sharing; other people can take the lead.
2. You develop your ear for hearing and learning melodies; you have time to think and listen while filling in a background.
3. Listeners will have different effects, etc., to listen to.

Back-up playing is an art in itself and can be the subject for another book. Here we'll explore what notes make up chords, some "oom-pah" chord background, and, most important, how to find some harmony notes for melodies you play.

First, a chord consists of three or more notes played simultaneously. Whoops! Problem already. How can you play three notes with two hammers? Some players have solved this with two-headed hammers, but we're going to bend the definition for our purposes. We'll play the chord in sections and, rather than get too technical, simply call what we play "a chord."

The big question is, "How do you determine what notes are in a chord?" Easy. We'll experiment with the key of G. Because we need room to work, following is two octaves of the scale (letter names, not notes).

G A B C D E F# G A B C D E F# G

A chord is built on each note in the scale; a G chord on the G note, and so forth. We need at least three notes for a chord, and choose the notes we need from the scale. We start with a note, then select every other note in the scale for a total of three to fill out the chord. For example:

A G chord is G B D. You start with G, skip A, take B, skip C and take D. The good news is, no matter what the key of any music you play, if you see the chord G over the music, the notes for the chord are G B D. The chord can be made different by the addition of a number or letters after the name.

Among the chords over the music in the book so far, you've seen "7" and "min" after some of the chord letters. The 7 denotes a four-tone chord instead of the typical three tones. A D7 chord is D F# A C.

The minor chord is denoted "m," "min," or "minor" after the letter. We're using "min" in this book. The best way to understand the difference between major and minor chords is to listen to their sounds.

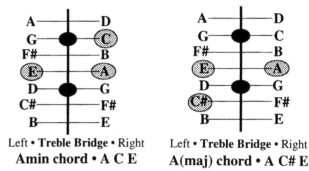

Left • **Treble Bridge** • Right
**Amin chord • A C E**

Left • **Treble Bridge** • Right
**A(maj) chord • A C# E**

*Please Note: Most of the chords you'll play are major chords. In music, major is the "default" scale and chord. Over the tunes in this book you'll see chords such as G and D and C and so forth. We don't have to define them as major chords. Any other chord (minors or 4-note chords, etc.) must be specific: Amin, G7, even Gmaj7. The chord above (A C# E) is simply an A chord; it's redundant to say A maj.*

If you are interested in the *structural* difference in major and minor chords, a music theory book will help. For those of you who know some music, I'll tell you that chords are constructed with a certain number of half-steps between the first and last tones. A piano is the best place to see the layout of half-steps; from any piano key to the next nearest key (black or white) is a half-step. The number of half-steps in a chord and where they're placed determines what are major, minor and more exotic chords. We'll discuss half-steps and some music structure later in the section on minor scales.

# Back-Up Chords

In lieu of another player, tape melodies in the book and back yourself up. Here's how. On the tunes in 2/4 or 4/4 time, play "oom-pah." Using the G chord as an example, this is G (oom) B/D (pah).

On the tunes in 3/4 time, play "oom-pah-pah." Again, using the G chord as an example, this is G (oom) B/D (pah) B/D (pah).

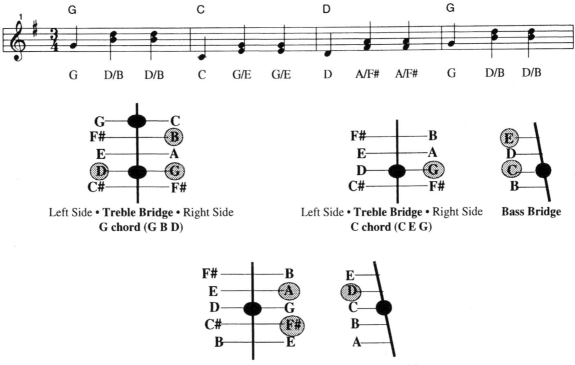

Following is the same chord sequence in the key of D. You will be playing more on the bass bridge this time.

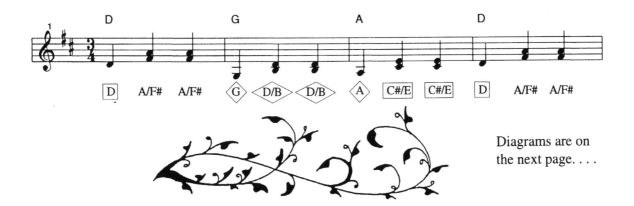

Diagrams are on
the next page. . . .

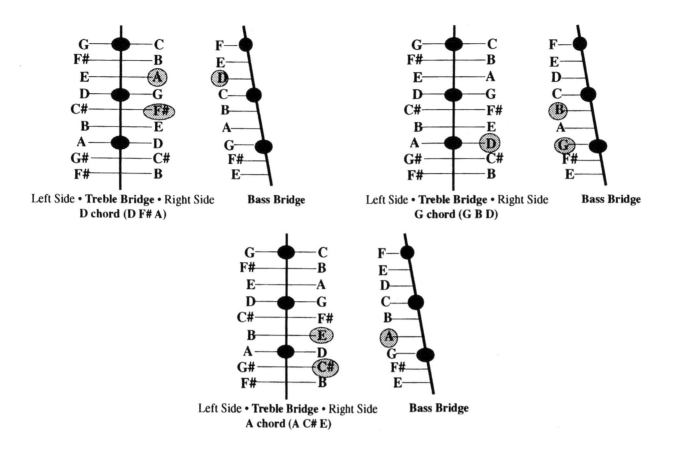

Left Side • **Treble Bridge** • Right Side
**D chord (D F# A)**

**Bass Bridge**

Left Side • **Treble Bridge** • Right Side
**G chord (G B D)**

**Bass Bridge**

Left Side • **Treble Bridge** • Right Side
**A chord (A C# E)**

**Bass Bridge**

**Something to notice:** The chords we use in the key of G are basically the same as those in the key of D. But, in the key of G we have a C chord while in the key of D we have an A chord. The two keys share the same notes except for the note C (in the key of G) and the note C# (in the key of D).

# Playing Chords in Different Note Orders

So far we've played the chords in the order of the notes (G, then B, then D for the G chord, for example). However, the notes can be mixed up (B, then D, then G, for example) and notes can be repeated (G, then B, then D, then G, for example). You can also leave out a note of the chord (G, then D, then G, for example).

Following are G chords in different positions. Try playing the notes individually (called an arpeggio) and by "oom pahs."

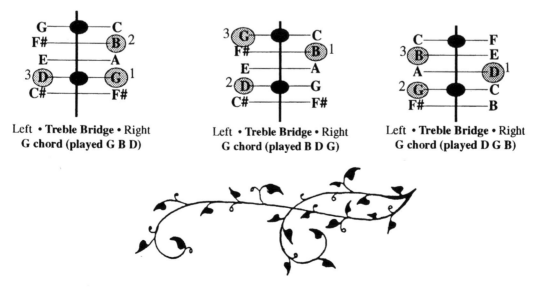

Left • **Treble Bridge** • Right
**G chord (played G B D)**

Left • **Treble Bridge** • Right
**G chord (played B D G)**

Left • **Treble Bridge** • Right
**G chord (played D G B)**

# Playing Chords by Shapes

Remember the diagram with the various keys blocked off? Your hammers make patterns as you play chords, and this can help you remember them, especially if you know the first note. Here are two primary shapes for chords that include a repeated first tone at the octave (G B D G, for example).

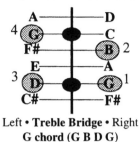

Left • **Treble Bridge** • Right
**G chord (G B D G)**

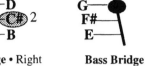

Left • **Treble Bridge** • Right          **Bass Bridge**
**A chord (A C# E A)**

See the blocky shape of this chord? Chords that are played on the treble bridge often look like this.

Chords that include the bass and treble bridges often have a diamond shape like this A chord.

# Learning Chords

Chord changes in a tune are not always predictable. Suppose you've just played "oom" and the chord changes on the next note. Flexibility is a sign of a good player. Because you're a good player (or getting there), you go to the next chord. Not as immediately easy as it reads, but in time it will happen.

Practice back-up chords at a festival or friendly jam session. If everything moves too fast for you, start or suggest a slow jam. Others more shy than you will be grateful! At jams you can always improve your rhythm, even if you don't know the melody, marking time by droning on the G, D or whatever notes sound good in the key being played in.

Sit near the guitarist and ask him or her for help in what chords are necessary. Watching the guitarist's hands for the changes is helpful. Back-up playing is one of the *best* teachers you can have.

# Chord Arpeggios
# Auld Lang Syne

Our primary goal with "Auld Lang Syne" is to practice *arpeggios*. Arpeggios are noticeable in the music because of the squiggly line to the left of a stack of notes. But, if a squiggly line is missing, and you have a stack of notes, they should be arpeggiated on the hammered dulcimer. You play an arpeggio by striking each note of a chord separately. You arpeggiate a G chord (G B D) by striking the G, then the B, followed by the D. You can mix up the notes in the arpeggio. For example, play B, then D, followed by G. Play the C arpeggio (diagram on the right) from the bottom up and then from the top down.

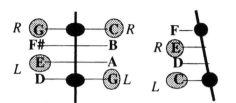

Left Side • **Treble Bridge** • Right Side      **Bass Bridge**

Example of a C arpeggio

Do you play an arpeggio quickly or slowly? The amount of rhythmic time (one beat, two beats, or more) you have to play the arpeggio answers that question. The arpeggios in measures 1 and 2 of "Auld Lang Syne" are short, for you have only a beat or a beat and a half to play them. Notice these arpeggios have three notes in them. The arpeggios in measures 4, 12, and 16 have three beats in which to play them, plenty of time to savor each note. Notice these arpeggios have five notes in them.

To play arpeggios you should alternate hammers and move horizontally when possible.

Arpeggios are tools to be used in your music. Please don't be tempted to play them continually in many tunes, on the first beat of each measure, for example. Too many of them obscure the melody and become predictable, almost boring.

Below are the four arpeggios found in measures 1 and 2 of "Auld Lang Syne." Work them out now before trying the tune. You begin the G, E minor, and A minor arpeggios on the bass bridge with the left hammer. You begin the D arpeggio on the bass bridge with the right hammer. The notes in the arpeggiated chords are not always in order and you end with the melody note. As a variation, try playing the melody note first and working backwards.

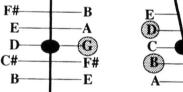

Left Side • **Treble Bridge** • Right Side      **Bass Bridge**
*G arpeggio, measure 1. Order of notes: B, D, G*

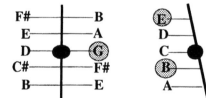

Left Side • **Treble Bridge** • Right Side      **Bass Bridge**
*Emin arpeggio, measure 1. Order of notes: B, E, G*

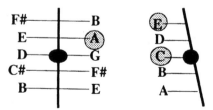

Left Side • **Treble Bridge** • Right Side      **Bass Bridge**
*Amin arpeggio, measure 1. Order of notes: C, E, A*

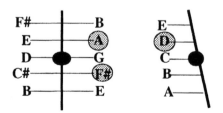

Left Side • **Treble Bridge** • Right Side      **Bass Bridge**
*D arpeggio, measure 1. Order of notes: D, F#, A*

# Auld Lang Syne

Scottish Melody

In measure 10, you'll have to play the second A (under the D chord) with your right hammer to catch the E with your left hammer.

The D and E (circled notes) are duplicated on the right and left sides of the treble bridge.

The note names under the arpeggios in the music are listed in the order in which you play the notes.

# F on the Bass Bridge, Bounces, Rolls, Fermatas
# My Own House

**Bass Bridge F:** "My Own House" introduces F on the bass bridge. That F (the note and the chord) makes the tune unique because the key of G has an F#, not an F-natural. D and E are found on both sides of the bridge and will help you with hammer patterns.

**Bounce:** Try the hammered dulcimer technique of bouncing hammers. The right hammer is the easiest to bounce, if you're right-handed. Hold the hammers loosely and let them drop on the strings. Your finger-tips control the bounce, ending it when you want. Try to put a bounce on the first note of *some* of the measures.

**Roll:** In some of the measures where the first note has a rhythmic value of two beats (measures 4 and 12 are suggestions), experiment with a controlled roll (think of a drum roll). Alternate the hammers on the melody note, filling in part of the two-beat space. Because this is a controlled move, and because both your left and right hammers need to work as one, a roll isn't as easy as a bounce. It's a useful technique, though, and worth the effort.

It is a temptation to use a bounce or a roll on the first beat of *every* measure once you learn how to do them. *Please don't!* Not only is this musically boring, you can obscure the melody.

**E-minor Arpeggio and a Fermata:** To the right is a playing scheme for the E-minor arpeggio near the end. You have two full beats; take your time playing the arpeggio. For a nice touch, you can hold the last note of the arpeggio before continuing. In written music, this hold is indicated by a *fermata* (belovedly called a "birds eye" by many musicians). Look at measure 28 to see a fermata on top of the arpeggio. But there's a temptation to hold the note too long at the end of the arpeggio. This can interrupt the flow of the music. Keep the tune moving by not lingering too long at the fermata.

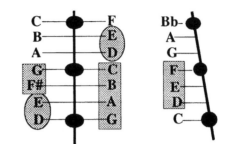

Left Side • **Treble Bridge** • Right Side    **Bass Bridge**

Notes in "My Own House"

Measure 28

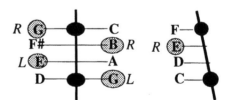

Left Side • **Treble Bridge** • Right Side    **Bass Bridge**

E-minor Arpeggio

# My Own House

Traditional Waltz

*Count Off: 1 Play*

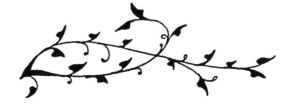

◇ Bass bridge
▭ Right side treble bridge
○ Left side treble bridge

# Triplets and more Interval Harmony Playing
# The Lark in the Clear Air

**Playing Suggestion:** If you want to play only the melody of "The Lark in the Clear Air," either at first or all of the time, ignore the stems-down notes; they are harmony.

Look at the tune. It uses the F# under G on the right side of the treble bridge. Sometimes, as in measure 9, this is a very quick visit. That is why a lot of this melody (even combined with the harmony) will be played vertically on the right side of the treble bridge. *In general,* the more a tune walks around (as opposed to jumps), the more vertical your hammering.

**Triplets:** The notes bracketed with a three are triplets. All three notes are played in the space of one beat. To practice, pat your leg in a 1-2-3-4 count. For each pat, quickly say, "dah—dah—dah." Because you're moving pretty fast on the triplets (even in this slow air), you *should* alternate hammers when playing through those sections.

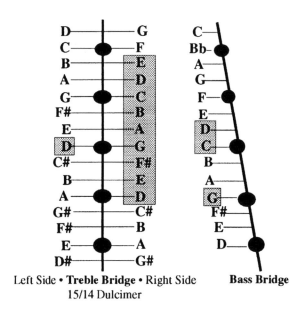

Left Side • **Treble Bridge** • Right Side
15/14 Dulcimer   **Bass Bridge**

**Hammering Suggestions:** Look at the melody (stems up). This tune jumps and walks and is generally active for a slow air. This means adaptability in hammering patterns. In measure 1 going to measure 2 you must go to the bass bridge for middle C. Once you're there, you might as well play the first D in measure 2 on the bass bridge. But, continuing in measure 2, you walk through an F# at the end. This means you should begin the walk (second D in measure 2) on the right side of the treble bridge. See what I mean about adapting your hammering to the situation?

# The Lark In The Clear Air

Irish Air

*Count Off: 1 Play*

♦ Bass bridge
☐ Right side treble bridge
◯ Left side treble bridge

# Horizontal Bass Bridge/Treble Bridge Moves
## Amazing Grace

"Amazing Grace" demonstrates a lot of horizontal right side treble bridge/bass bridge moving. If your hands are close together you can observe what they're doing (striking right notes)! The first D in the tune should be played on the bass bridge, as should the last note in measures 4 and 12.

An example of the horizontal harmony movement happens in measure 10 going to 11. The melody notes are played on the right side of the treble bridge while the harmony notes are played on the bass bridge. This keeps your hands close.

Remember how 3rd intervals should be played vertically? There is an exception in measure 3, repeated in measure 11. You begin the measure with a 5th interval G and C (horizontal), go to a 3rd interval E and C (still horizontal), and end the harmony section with a 5th interval D and G in measure 4 (horizontal). Playing the whole section horizontally keeps movement to a minimum.

**Review — F on the Bass Bridge:** The key of G has an F#. To make an interesting harmony in measures 2 and 9, we're going to play an F-natural with the B. The F-natural is found only on the bass bridge and is marked on the diagram.

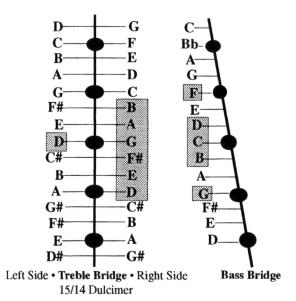

Left Side • **Treble Bridge** • Right Side
15/14 Dulcimer

**Bass Bridge**

**D Arpeggio in measure 7:** Begin on the bass bridge D, move to F# and A on the right side of the treble bridge, and end with the D on the left side.

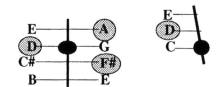

Left Side • **Treble Bridge** • Right Side  **Bass Bridge**

D arpeggio

> *If you prefer, play only the melody (top notes) and ignore the harmony (bottom notes). Both melody and harmony notes are on the same stem.*

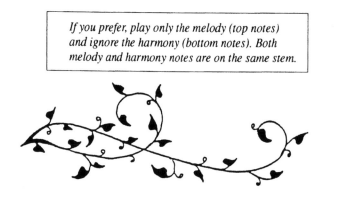

# Amazing Grace

from Virginia Harmony (19th Cent.)

words by John Newton

*Count Off: 1 Play*

◇ Bass bridge
▢ Right side treble bridge
◯ Left side treble bridge

# Review: Hornpipes, Triplets, Transitional Notes
# Off To California

**Review — Hornpipes:** Remember the long-short feel in playing a hornpipe? To refresh your memory, review the hornpipe "Harvest Home" on pages 38 and 39.

**Review — Triplets:** If necessary, review triplets as we used them in "The Lark in the Clear Air" on pages 58 and 59.

**Review — Transitional Notes:** We've spoken of duplicated and transitional notes on the dulcimer. You can review them in this tune. I've marked two B's with circles on the diagram. If you start this tune with the right hammer, alternating, you get to the B (second note in measure 2) and it is more convenient to play it on the right side. If you begin with the left hammer, however, it is more convenient to cross to the left side for that B.

Suppose you have a C D E F# *treble bridge* passage in a tune. The C is only on the right side, the F# is only on the left side, but the D and E are on both sides. You decide where to play the D, and possible the E, by whatever hammer you're using at that point.

**Practice the following:** Map your way through measure 3 of "Off To California." You must stay on the left side for the two Gs and the F#, but you can cross to the right side on the 4th note, the 7th note or the 8th note (awkward move). Which works easiest for you? The hammering suggestions I've put in the music are simply that — suggestions. Write in any of your revisions.

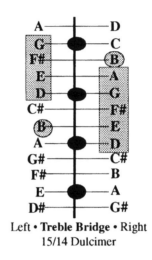

Left • **Treble Bridge** • Right
15/14 Dulcimer

If you don't read music (and even if you do), "Off To California" might look daunting at first. But, measures 5–8 repeat measures 1–4 (except for one note at the end of measure 8). Then measures 13–16 are similar to measures 5–8. Work the tune out through measure 4 (follow the measure numbers) and the rest of the tune will be easier.

# Off To California

*Count Off: 1 Ready Play*

Irish Hornpipe

# Drone Harmony
# Soldier's Joy

"Soldier's Joy" is a staple at old-time music jam sessions. You'll hear as many variations as there are players. Some are less ornate than this arrangement; some are more. As you become more familiar with your dulcimer and how to play it, you can provide your own arrangement.

**Drone:** A drone is a continually repeated note filling in a background. To use one in this tune, play the A (circled on the diagram) as a harmony note on beat 1 in measures 9, 10, 11, 13, and 14. Measures 9 and 10 are exampled below. For a nice sound, bounce your hammer on the drone A.

Playing Suggestion: In the arrangement of "Harvest Home," I suggested you play the first measure (consisting of D's, F#'s and A's) vertically on the right side of the treble bridge. In "Soldiers' Joy," I suggest you play the D's and F#'s on the right side and the A's on the left side in measures 1, 3, and 5. Beginning the tune with the left hammer sets up a nice toggle back and forth from the left side to the right side of the treble bridge.

A lot of "Soldier's Joy" is played on the left side of the treble bridge, including all of measures 9 through 16 (melody). Remember to sit or stand centered at the treble bridge of the dulcimer and the long passages on the left side of the treble bridge will be easier to play.

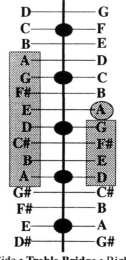

Left Side • **Treble Bridge** • Right Side
15/14 Dulcimer

"Soldier's Joy," being a standard fiddle tune,  is played with repeats. Play from the beginning through measure 8 twice and then play measures 9 through 16 twice. Remember that your repeat guides are the dots by the bar lines in measures 8, 9 and 16.

# Soldier's Joy

*Count Off: 1 Ready Play*

Traditional Fiddle Tune

# Minor Keys

So far we've worked with major scales; minor scales are next. The hammered dulcimer neatly organizes major and minor scales, but first we'll study briefly what makes them different from each other.

The smallest interval in music familiar throughout most of the world is a half-step. To see half-steps, look at this diagram of a piano keyboard. You don't have to be able to play the piano!

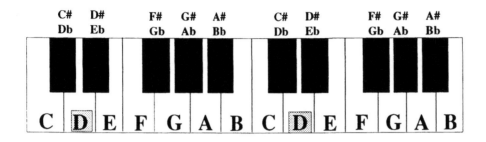

The smallest step you can take on the piano — to the nearest black or white key — is a half-step. The octave D to D (marked on the diagram) holds twelve half-steps. To make major and minor scales we take the twelve half-steps and combine them into a combination of two half-steps and five whole-steps.

The **major scale pattern** is:
whole-step • whole-step • half-step • whole-step • whole-step • whole-step • half-step

The D (major) scale is
D E F# G A B C# D

Remember that major is the "default." If we say key of D or the D scale, major is implied. Using the major scale pattern and the keyboard diagram, figure out the notes in several scales — G, C, and A, for example.

**Minor scales** over the centuries have been modified to create variations. We'll concentrate on the natural minor, the pattern of which is:
whole-step • half-step • whole-step • whole-step • half-step • whole-step • whole-step

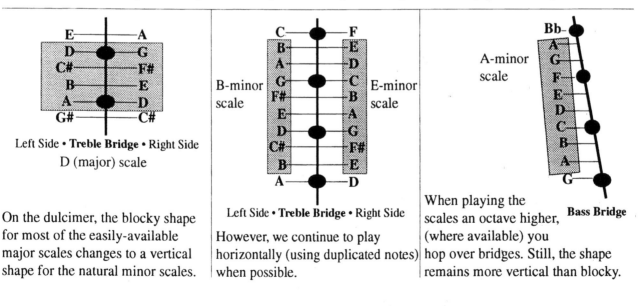

Left Side • **Treble Bridge** • Right Side
D (major) scale

Left Side • **Treble Bridge** • Right Side

A-minor scale

**Bass Bridge**

On the dulcimer, the blocky shape for most of the easily-available major scales changes to a vertical shape for the natural minor scales.

However, we continue to play horizontally (using duplicated notes) when possible.

When playing the scales an octave higher, (where available) you hop over bridges. Still, the shape remains more vertical than blocky.

66

# The Parting Glass

◇ Bass bridge
☐ Right side treble bridge
◯ Left side treble bridge

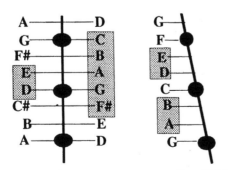

Left Side • **Treble Bridge** • Right Side    **Bass Bridge**

The key of E minor is so beautiful; it is a favorite key of mine. Even though you find the natural scale running from E to E on the right side of the treble bridge, we'll work horizontally a lot, owing to duplicated notes and the 4ths and 5ths in the interval harmony.

# Star of the County Down

Irish Air

*Count Off: 1 Ready Play*

♩ = *112*

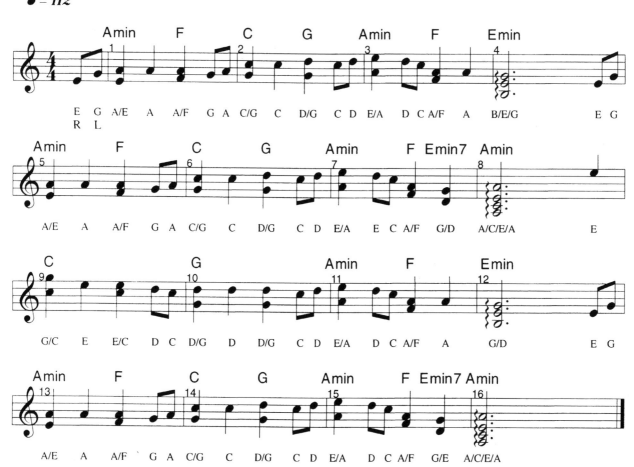

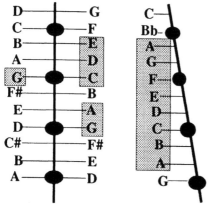

**Left • Treble Bridge • Right**          **Bass Bridge**

This exquisite air uses a lovely section of the dulcimer: A-minor, found mainly on the bass bridge. Remind yourself of the A-minor scale, pictured in the section on minor scales, by playing through it a few times.

A lot of the intervals are shared between the bass bridge and the right side of the treble bridge. Because some dulcimers do not have a high G on the right side of the treble bridge, I opt for it on the left side. Actually, using that left G in measure 9 gives you a nice horizontal 5th interval.

# Practice Tune

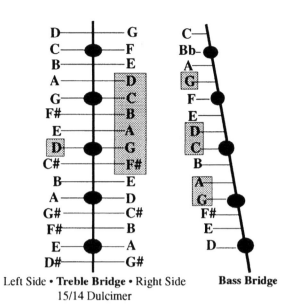

Left Side • **Treble Bridge** • Right Side
15/14 Dulcimer

**Bass Bridge**

This is not an easy arrangement. This is a familiar tune, however, and that will help you. Play the melody a few time (stems up) until it feels comfortable. Do not lock yourself into hammering patterns you can't change, for a lot will change when you add the harmony notes. To learn the melody and harmony together, I suggest you take small sections (a measure or two). Put in the harmony now and then, as it feels comfortable. If it takes you several months to put it all together, that's all right.

Look at measures 2, 11 and 14. Similar things are happening as you approach a 5th interval harmony on D and G. You'll want to play the D and G horizontally, but you have a choice. You can play D on the left side of the treble bridge and G on the right, or G on the upper part of the bass bridge and D on the right side of the treble bridge. Both work.

# Simple Gifts

Shaker Song

◇ Bass bridge
▭ Right side treble bridge
◯ Left side treble bridge

69

# Modulation

Be of good cheer. Even though the first, second or fifth reading of the explanation of a typical modulation might leave you counting on your fingers and saying, "Run that by me again," you've probably already played some tunes with modulations. *A modulation simply takes you to a new key and, usually, back to the original.* The new key can be used in an entire section ("Flop-Eared Mule" is an example) or in a few measures ("The Ash Grove"). The modulations that might have sneaked by you are the short ones. Here's how modulations work. The most common brief modulation is from the current key (also called the tonic key) to the dominant key, which is based on the fifth tone of the tonic key. You get there through the dominant chord (based on the fifth tone) of the new key! As I've emphasized before, there is a strong relationship of one to five, be they notes in a scale, in a chord or, now, a key.

We're going to modulate from the key of G to the key of D, as an example. First, look at the scales.

*The G Scale:*  G A B C D E F# G
*The D Scale:*  D E F# G A B C# D

Following is a chord series modulating from the key of G to the key of D. Listen to the sound.

*How do you get back to the original key? Or do you?* Most of the time you *do* go back to the original key. In our example, we'll go from the key of G to the key of D and back again.

For a further understanding of modulation, compare the example keys of G and D above. Except for the note C, they both use the same notes (albeit in a different order). In the key of G, the C is C-natural; in the key of D, it is C#. To get from the key of G to the key of D, we have to introduce a C#.

Play the following sequence. It starts in the key of G, goes to the key of D, and returns to G — all by introducing a C# and then going back to a C-natural.

Following is a modulation in the key of D. The scale is D E F# G A B C# D, with A being the fifth tone. You're going to the key of A by way of an E chord. The notes in an E chord are E G# B, enabling us to add a G#, which is necessary in the key of A.

"Flop-Eared Mule" exemplifies a tune in the key of D modulating to A. "The Ash Grove" is in the key of G and modulates briefly to the key of D.

# Flop-Eared Mule

*Count Off: 1-2 Ready Play*

American Fiddle Tune

◇ Bass bridge
▢ Right side treble bridge
◯ Left side treble bridge

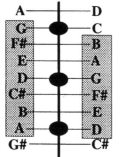

Left Side • **Treble Bridge** • Right Side

"Flop-Eared Mule" is an example of a tune that modulates; but it doesn't modulate in a typical fashion. One entire section is played in another key (A) and you don't get there through any fancy chord changes; you just go. Measures 9 through 16 are in the key of A.

# Musical Form and Another Modulation
# Over The Waterfall

There's lots to study in this basically easy, fun-to-play-tune. "Over The Waterfall" is a staple at old-time music jams.

**Musical Form:** We've spoken before of repeats and dots next to bar lines. A lot of words can boil down to, Play the tune AABB. You play eight measures, repeat them, play the next eight measures and repeat those. We're talking *full* measures, so follow the measure numbers. *Many* of the tunes you'll play on the dulcimer have a form of AABB.

Then each section breaks down into a little form of its own: two-measure segments. Imagine sentences becoming paragraphs. Some of the segments are repeated, helping you to learn the tune. Breaking down the A and B sections into two-measure segments, we have (using W, X, Y and Z) W, W1, W, X then Y, Y1, Y, Z.

To explain: a little melody is stated (measures 1 and 2). Measures 3 and 4 change that melody slightly. Measures 5 and 6 repeat measures 1 and 2, while measures 7 and 8 are very different from any of the other measures. Understanding how little sections go together to make big sections helps you learn long tunes a lot easier. Think of some tunes you know. Hum or play them, thinking about how they go together. Look at a piece of music. Even if you're not a fast reader, you can usually see repeated sections and measures that are the same or similar.

Return to "Flop-Eared Mule" and study its form: ABA. Measures 1–8 are section A, measures 9–16 are section B, and measures 17–24 repeat measures 1–8 (section A).

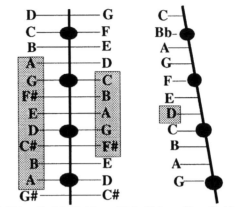

Left Side • **Treble Bridge** • Right Side    **Bass Bridge**

**Modulation:** This tune modulates from the key of D to the key of G. This is a little unusual, since most tunes modulating from D go to the key of A. This time we have to get rid of the C# (in the key of D), and replace it with a C (for the key of G) . We do this in measure 7.

**Vertical runs:** If you're right-handed, the easiest place to play vertical runs in the tune is on the right side of the treble bridge, followed, perhaps, by the bass bridge. You have several left-side treble bridge runs in this tune; good practice!

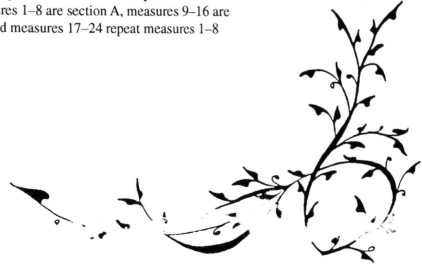

# Over The Waterfall

Traditional American Fiddle Tune

*Count Off: 1 Ready Play*

♩ = **192**

# Another Modulation and 3rd Interval Harmony
# The Ash Grove

"The Ash Grove" has its difficult spots. You might play just the melody first to get the tune in your mind before trying melody and harmony together.

**Modulation:** Measures 23 and 24 have a modulation from the key of G to the key of D. See how the C# necessary for the key of D is added into the melody? Sometimes a melody doesn't indicate a modulation (no out-of-scale notes), but the harmony does. This time melody and harmony both work through the modulation. Look at the chords over the melody in measures 23 and 24. As with most typical modulations, it just seems that something is happening!

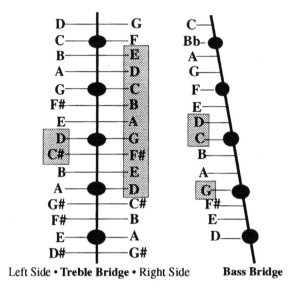

Left Side • **Treble Bridge** • Right Side          **Bass Bridge**

**A String of 3rds:** All of the notes in the section with 3rds should be played on the right side of the treble bridge. *Play vertically.* Once you know the basic melody and harmony, keep telling yourself to relax, hang loose — and be cool — through the long section of thirds. Don't tighten up!

# The Ash Grove

Traditional Welsh Song

75

# O'Carolan, Planxties, Walking Harmony Bass Line
# Planxty Fanny Po'er

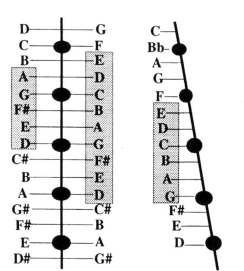

```
D———————G        C—
C———————F        Bb-
B———————E        A—
A———————D        G—
G———————C        F—
F#——————B        E—
E———————A        D—
D———————G        C—
C#——————F#       B—
B———————E        A—
A———————D        G—
G#——————C#       F#
F#——————B        E—
E———————A        D—
D#——————G#
```

Left Side • **Treble Bridge** • Right Side      **Bass Bridge**

A hammered dulcimer book wouldn't be complete without a piece by Ireland's Turlough O'Carolan (1670-1738). Most dulcimer players have at least one piece of his in their repertoire.

O'Carolan lost his sight as a teenager, learned to play the Celtic harp, and spent the rest of his life performing and writing music for his patrons. These gifts in honor of his patrons are planxties. About 200 of his melodies have come down to us, and you can find books of them, as well as selections in some Irish tunebooks.

"Planxty Fanny Po'er" is a great melody with or without the harmony. Parts of the harmony are fairly difficult, especially in measures 9 through 16. In measures 11 through 14 the harmony notes are located far from the melody. Because the melody goes high and because I like consistency in an arrangement (harmony stays in the same range), the distance is necessary. If it is too difficult, move the harmony up an octave.

Look at the harmony (stems down) from measure 9 to the beginning of measure 12. This is a walking harmony. It walks down the scale almost a full octave. Chords in that section look different. G/F#, for example, means a G chord with an F# on the bass. You probably know there isn't an F# in a G chord, but you add it in to walk you to the E in the E-minor chord. These chord variations provide interesting sounds. Watch a bass player some time. They are famous for their walking bass lines.

# Planxty Fanny Po'er

Turlough O'Carolan (1670-1738)

*Count Off: 1-2-3 4-5 (enter on 6)*

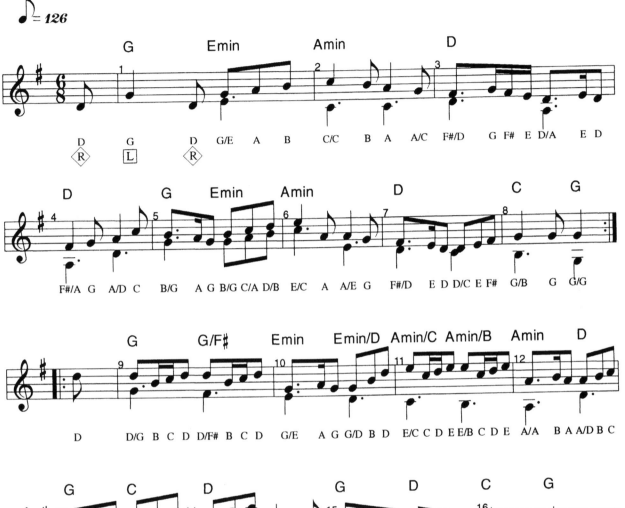

◇ Bass bridge
▢ Right side treble bridge
○ Left side treble bridge

# The Key of A, Adapting Music to the Dulcimer, Jigs
# The Hundred Pipers

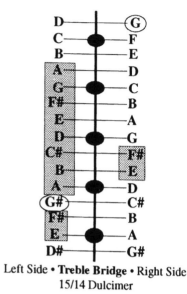

Left Side • **Treble Bridge** • Right Side
15/14 Dulcimer

**The Key of A:** Fiddlers like the key of A, so here's a tune for a jam session that includes fiddlers! Playing in the key of A means you'll use the left side of the treble bridge a lot. Notice that a 15/14 dulcimer has an A scale at the bottom. Smaller dulcimers have the key of A, but you need to hop the bridges more. Both the 15/14 and 12/11 dulcimers have a problem with the high octave of the key of A. The A scale is A B C# D E F# G# A. Most dulcimers don't have a high G#, although most dulcimers do have a low G# (circled on the diagram). I've also circled the G at the very top of the right side of the treble bridge. Chromatic and extended range dulcimers generally have a high G# there. Even some of the 15/14 dulcimers have that G#. However, this tune doesn't need the high G#, so we're fine.

**Adapting Music:** But, if you needed the high G♯ for a tune, you could either alter the melody (we're going to do that in "Jesu, Joy of Man's Desiring") or try dropping all or part of the melody an octave lower. To drop the melody lower, in some cases, you might need a 15/14 dulcimer.

**Especially for 15/14 Dulcimers:** If you have a 15/14 dulcimer the E and F♯ on the right side of the treble bridge are duplicated on the left side near the bottom. Remember them if you want them for your hammering patterns.

**Jigs:** The last thing to mention is 6/8 time, sometimes called "jig time." Say, "jiggity, jiggity" to get a feeling of the rhythm. A jig doesn't have to be at break-neck speed, by the way. It does, however, need the dance feeling — it's a dance rhythm.

# The Hundred Pipers

*Count Off: 1-2-3 4-5 (enter on 6)*

Traditional Jig

♪ = 116

◇ Bass bridge
▢ Right side treble bridge
◯ Left side treble bridge

# Santa Lucia

Italian Boat Song

Count Off: 1 Ready Play

◇ Bass bridge
☐ Right side treble bridge
◯ Left side treble bridge

"Santa Lucia" presents an out-of-key tone (the G#) and a little chromatic run. Chromatic simply means moving along via half steps. Since the hammered dulcimer isn't *set up* as a chromatic instrument (the chromatic notes are there, but not always close to each other), you have to jump around to get out-of-key notes. In this case, you go to the bottom left of your dulcimer to catch the A and the G#, then hop back to the right side for the G.

Left Side • **Treble Bridge** • Right Side

80

# Playing Music With Style

## Musical Nuances

**Tremolo:** Players of the cousins of hammerd dulcimers have techniques that translate well on the dulcimer. The best way for you to explore the instrument fully is to listen to recordings (or live players) of such instruments as the cymbalom (Hungary) and the hackbrett (Germany). You can also learn from xylophone and marimba players. One technique used frequently, particularly on the cymbalom, xylophone and marimba, is the tremolo. That is a continuous rapid right/left hammer bounce on one pitch or two. A tremolo on a sixth interval is particularly nice. Imagine the tremolo stop on a pipe organ and try to recreate that on the dulcimer. The tremolo effect sounds nice as an accent in waltzes.

**Harmonics:** On the left side of the treble bridge you are able to play courses farther from the bridge. (On the right side, you have to avoid the courses coming from the bass bridge.) By striking the left-bridge course about two-and-a-half inches from the bridge (approximately half way between the bridge and the side bridge) you can achieve bell-like tones close to the sound of bells or harmonics. I find the higher notes particularly nice. Use these harmonic-like sounds anytime you want to imitate a bell; the last note or two of a tune is a nice spot for this technique.

**Phrasing:** But before a melody needs harmony, it should stand alone, unadorned, and sing beautifully by itself. There are all kinds of adjectives to describe a tune — among them sprightly, pensive, fluid, bright — but sooner or later they all come down to phrasing.

Think of a dulcimer player whose music you especially enjoy. In all probability listening to his or her music moves you to some physical action: swaying, dancing, etc. Among other things, you are reacting to the player's phrasing.

In a verbal sense, consider the following question. "How are you today?" Read that sentence with various accents.

> How are you *today*?
> How *are* you today?
> How are *you* today?
> *How* are you today?

Combine the accents with volume or even your concern for the answer. Consider the casual inquiry by a clerk in a store compared with a friend's concern after you've been ill.

**Creativity:** After our discussions of half-steps and quarter notes and other left-brain items, here is something with which you've worked all of your life. Suppose you cook very well and I ask you why your mushroom barley soup tastes so good. In all probability you tell me the primary difference is "a little bit of this and a little bit of that." I might take the mushrooms and barley and other ingredients, read the recipe, consider a quarter teaspoon of something to be exactly that, and get something predictable. You'd probably gauge the textures of the vegetables, add a pinch more (or less) of something, and get a distinctive soup. If you are creative with knitting or cooking or woodwork or painting or gardening, try using that creativity with music.

When you know a tune somewhat, you can make the *sounding* of one phrase different from the other. This is where words such as sprightly and pensive and moody and bright help you. If you consider a tune to be one danced by children and I consider it one that reminds me of sunlight dancing in trees, we'll get different results from the writer of the tune—who was thinking of leprechauns!

It is much easier to tell you to strike this note with this hammer or that a D major scale is always D E F# G A B C# D. However, as you learn the mechanical aspects of music and the dulcimer, let your feelings come forth. Many people think, "Well, when I can *play* the instrument, *then* I'll play the music with feeling." Don't be one of them! Play with feeling from the beginning.

If you see "Soldier's Joy" in a fiddle book with a caption saying that it's from the playing of Joe Smith as recorded in North Carolina in 1957, that was the way Joe Smith played the tune while the microphone was under his nose. I dare say the next day he played it differently.

The style of a player is learned by sitting at his or her feet for *many* hours. The collectors didn't just stop by for a cup of coffee and a tune. Often friendship bonds were established as collector and musician chronicled musical history. To understand how Joe Smith approached tunes like "Soldier's Joy" the collector/archivist didn't just record the tune once, write it down, and say this is the one true way in which to play it. We're talking musical expression, which changes the more a player grows with his or her music. As you

continue to play the dulcimer, and allow yourself flexibility, you'll be able to take a new tune and develop it by letting your personality come through. Working with written music, this can happen simply by putting the music away and playing the tune as you feel it.

**Memorizing Music:** Here are four thoughts to help you translate written music to your hands.

• Start somewhere rather than the beginning of
        a tune when you practice.
• If you get lost, don't stop! If you are hopelessly lost,
        work out the section that tripped you up so it is
        less likely to happen again.
• Recognize repeated sections and sections that are
        very similar but different.
• Memorize small sections starting with the *last*
        measure. Somehow the beginning is always
        easier!

# Jesu, Joy of Man's Desiring

After all your work, we've come to the end of the book. A lot of dulcimer players want to play "Jesu, Joy of Man's Desiring," so I leave you with it. Yes, it looks long. But, so many of the musical ideas and skills we've developed meet in this arrangement. There are repeated sections, interval harmony and even out of-key notes. Again, I suggest you approach "Jesu" in small bites.

There are some things to discuss. First, you may be new to 9/8 time. It is very similar to 3/4 time, as the eighth notes group together in three sets of three. Count a portion of the melody out a few times and you should get the feel of it.

Measures 41 through 52 have lots of out-of-key notes that will keep you hopping. If you find this section prevents you from playing "Jesu, Joy of Man's Desiring," please alter the arrangement. I've heard several dulcimer players who leave out that section. It is, however, very nice and takes you through interesting modulations.

In measure 45 (third note) there is a high G#. Your dulcimer might not have one. If it does, it's probably located at or near the top of the right side of the treble bridge. If you don't have the G#, play a B instead. This will make the measure play E A B A E C A B C instead of E A G# A E C A B C.

# Jesu, Joy of Man's Desiring

*Count Off: 1 (enter on 2)*

Johann Sebastian Bach (1685-1750)

♩. = 76

F#ACDBGEGB CAF#DF#ACB GBDCCEDDG F#GF#GDBGAB CDEDCBABG

F#GADF#ACBA BGABDCCED DGF#GDBGAB EDCBAGDGF# GBDG

# In Closing

## Musical Profiles

You've heard, I'm sure, of people who are considered talented musically or of others who can't carry a tune in a bucket. These blanket statements shouldn't cover us. We're assembled intricately in music! In this book we've studied melody, rhythm, harmony, and musical form. Suppose you draw a diagram of your musical abilities using those four guides. Do you find yourself responding to the rhythm of a piece of music, particularly in a physical way such as drumming on a table? You have the gift of rhythm. If someone sings you a tune, do you pick it up right away and find yourself humming it for hours later? You have the gift of melody. If someone plays a melody, do you want to put some harmony in it somewhere? You have the gift of harmony. Do you recognize how music seems to go together, anticipating repeated sections and endings? You have the gift of form.

Recognizing your strengths and weaknesses can help you learn the dulcimer. If you can't seem to establish or keep the beat, perhaps a drumming class is in order. It matters not if the teacher has never heard of a hammered dulcimer; you are there to pull out some of the rhythm within you and use it on your instrument. If you find that melodies are easy for you but they're not translating into interesting arrangements on your dulcimer, playing backup in jam sessions (entire jam sessions!) could eventually bring you more ease with harmony.

I am a very harmonic player. I've sung all of my life and enjoy using the dulcimer as an accompanying instrument. My dulcimer playing style leans heavily on harmony. Yet, I've had to work on developing a rhythmic sense. To this day, it is hard for me to retain melodies when I first hear them. I try to organize melodies in my head (high, low, jumps) to build that part of my musical profile.

Interestingly, I believe one way a person can develop a sense of form within themselves is to study (participating or as an observer) dance or poetry. Form is important in developing musical programs, should you wish to perform.

As you examine books of dulcimer music or instruction, try to determine the teacher or arranger's musical profile. Sometimes a teacher's musical approach should mesh with yours; sometimes it is good to venture off in another direction.

## An Arrangement Is Never Complete

Please don't lock any doors on yourself. I once heard someone speaking about dreams. He said, "If you decide totally what the dream means it can no longer teach you." If you have the definitive way to play a tune, it can no longer teach you. A favorite piece of mine is the song "Shenandoah." I've probably performed that song more than any other I know. Each time there's a difference, reflecting my place at the moment. Am I singing the song for people who live in Virginia's Shenandoah Valley? Have they probably never been here? Is this a new audience or one for whom I've performed several times? Even when I commit something to paper, it can change hours later as a new thought enters my mind. Never close the door on any part of your musical learning.

## Dulcimer Players News

I'd be remiss if I didn't mention *Dulcimer Players News,* which began publication in 1975. This quarterly publication will give you information about festivals, workshops, clubs, new books and recordings, players, builders and dulcimer news in general. I recommend it to you, but demurely, since I'm the publisher/editor! No matter, it will be a good resource for you. The address is PO Box 2164, Winchester, VA 22604. Phone 540/678-1305.

## Last thought

A teacher friend, Jane Comfort Brown, once shared this saying by our good companion Anonymous: "Continuous improvement is better than postponed perfection." Play the music, learn from it and then share it with others, even if only through your appreciation. Thank you for inviting me to share your musical journey!

In harmony,

*Maddie Marvel*

*Great Music at Your Fingertips*